Reclaimers

Reclaimers

Ana Maria Spagna

UNIVERSITY OF WASHINGTON PRESS

Seattle and London

UNIVERSITY OF WASHINGTON PRESS
www.washington.edu/uwpress

LIBRARY OF CONGRESS CATALOGING-IN-PUBLICATION DATA
Spagna, Ana Maria.
Reclaimers / Ana Maria Spagna.
     pages cm
ISBN 978-0-295-99513-7 (hardback : alk. paper)
1. Northwest, Pacific—Environmental conditions.
2. Environmental protection—Northwest, Pacific.
3. Reclamation of land—Northwest, Pacific.
4. Women environmentalists—Northwest, Pacific—Biography.
5. Northwest, Pacific—Biography.
6. Indians of North America—Land tenure—Northwest, Pacific.
7. Mountains—Environmental aspects—Northwest, Pacific.
8. Rivers—Environmental aspects—Northwest, Pacific.
9. Northwest, Pacific—Description and travel.
10. Spagna, Ana Maria—Travel—Northwest, Pacific.
I. Title.
GE155.N75S62 2015   333.71'5309795—dc23   2015011382

DISCARD

Contents

Prologue

The Low Ground

 Thehe two-acre property my wife, Laurie, and I own in Stehekin, a very small mountain town, divides cleanly in two: the high ground where we live now, atop an ancient moraine, and the low ground, where we lived years ago. In many ways, the halves are the same. Same trees. Same gravel road perimeter. Same mossy rocks. But while the high ground, these days, appears well-groomed—native shrubs line the driveway, high-limbed firs filter sunlight, a fourteen-hundred-square-foot cabin stretches the definition—the low ground has gone feral: crisscrossed with downed cottonwoods, littered with flood-strewn lumber, silty and splintered, discarded skis, rock rubble, and for a time, an unclaimed motorcycle helmet perched on a stump. No dwellings. Not anymore. One lone structure, a ramshackle garage half-sided and rat-infested, remains at the far end of the plat. We still use it for storage, so to retrieve our winter boots or a blow-up boat or a coffee can of lag screws, we must head down. But for a long time, I avoided the chore at all costs: procrastinating, excuse-making, dreading the sight of ground, supposedly our own, flushed, scoured, trashed, abandoned.

Truth is, the low ground was never much to brag about. When Laurie's mother first saw the place, she wept. For good reason. A rusted off-kilter swing set lay in the yard alongside hardened bags of mortar, stockpiles of broken brick, and several untended outbuildings. Brush filled in the gaps: thimbleberries and Oregon grape and fireweed, all of it brown with road dust. The former owners, a family of seven, had lived in a small unfinished house sided with T1-11, and they'd made a hard go of it: a woodshed, a garden, a smokehouse, and a hog pen. They fled when a November flood brought the river charging to the doorstep, seeping through floorboards. They were rescued in the bucket of a front-end loader, and soon put the place on the market. And we, knowing all this, spent our life savings to buy it.

We had reason to weep, but we never did. We worked instead, the way only earnest new landowners can. We were used to manual labor—both Laurie and I had worked for years, by then, on backcountry trail crews for the National Park Service and the U.S. Forest Service, and Laurie still worked for the Park Service maintaining a historic apple orchard in the valley—and we were enamored, despite our left-leaning politics and our meager means, of the American Dream. We planned, eventually, to move to high ground, safely away from the danger of floods, but in the meantime we tore out moldy carpet and started anew: plumbing, insulating, stacking wood. We even planted a garden or, I should say, replanted the one that had washed to rubble in that November flood, then gone to weeds in one fallow summer. Reclaimed it, you might say.

We dug in cedar posts and spent $300—a small fortune at the time—on concrete mesh, strung it eight feet high to keep the deer and bear out, and added compost and minerals to the rocky soil. One day when I was preparing to plant potatoes, the neighbor's cat, Daisy, nudged up beside me, reared up on her hind paws, and began to dig full bore. With no idea what the purpose was, she threw herself at the task. I'm telling you: she was one of us, this cat.

That was seventeen years ago now, but it seems so much longer. Floods ripped through the low ground not once but three times, leaving firewood scattered, cedar posts askew. Soil from the garden washed downvalley to fertilize brambles that finger now through misshapen rolls of mesh. We left the house empty, and we skedaddled. Daisy moved with us, trailing us to high ground with the neighbors' blessing, claiming us and gifted to us both. Each fall I stand boot-tangled in blackberries to buck former cedar fence posts into chunks to split for kindling and fight a gnawing sense of loss.

But what did we lose? Not our lives, not our property. A neighbor couple had to sell off their flooded land, their summer home for over fifty years, to the government since there'd be no way to avoid future floods and likely no willing private buyers. We lost nothing, really, other than three hundred bucks, a garden spot, and a few thousand hours of labor. Still I wonder: Was it worth it? What was it all for? Sometimes I can't face the low ground. Even though it's what we planned to see happen, even though I love that David Byrne song about parking lots turning to daisies with a passion, I can't face it. Sometimes I need to get the hell out.

What happened on the low ground—what we accomplished, what we failed to accomplish, what, if anything, we need to reaccomplish—is what first got me thinking about reclamation. As long as I could remember, I thought the word had only to do with dams. The Bureau of Reclamation. Founded in 1902, tasked with reclaiming the arid West, making the desert bloom, building dams, dams, dams. By the late 1980s, when I landed in an auditorium-packed environmental studies class at college, the word held the scourge of outmoded arrogance: concrete oversized turbines, men with dress shirts stretched tight over their bellies, slide rules in their pockets, and god on their side. John McPhee's *Encounters with the Archdruid* provided the prototype in Floyd Dominy, longtime commissioner of the Bureau. A few years later, when I landed on trail crew, a job that required stubborn work-in-the-dirt contrariness, I began to see outmoded arrogance in the counterview as well. Marc Reisner's *Cadillac Desert* had predicted catastrophes of siltation that never quite materialized, not yet at least. Then there was Dominy's antagonist in *Archdruid*, environmental superhero David Brower, whose crusade to save the Colorado River in the Grand Canyon from proposed dams in the 1960s, laudable as it was, offers little insight on how to provide water to the millions of people who've since flocked to the Southwest. When I taught *Archdruid* to college freshmen in the 1990s, mostly from suburban Phoenix, they approached the entire controversy with head-scratching befuddlement. After three full weeks, one young woman, one of the best students in the class, raised her hand to ask: How do they decide which side of the dam the lake goes on?

I realized, then, that I'd omitted some crucial content, and also how little any of us understand the whole concept.

I looked up a definition.

Reclaim:

1. to recall from wrong or improper conduct
2. to rescue from an undesirable state; *also* : to restore to a previous natural state <*reclaim* mining sites> *b* : to make available for human use by changing natural conditions <*reclaim* swampland>

What is wrong or improper conduct when it comes to the natural world? What is an undesirable state? Where is the moral high ground? (Or, for that matter, the low ground?) And who decides? Judgments cycle. Fire is bad, fire is good. Predators are bad, predators are good. And with the judgments, so go our actions: Put out fires, start prescribed fires. Eliminate predators, reintroduce predators. Like Sisyphus on a hamster wheel. More to the point, aren't at least two of those definitions at odds with one another: to restore to a natural state and to make available for human use?

Still, what was most beguiling about the word was also what appealed to me. At some point in our recent history, and with good reason, a lot of us, the nature-minded, had become distrustful about messing with forests or floodplains or fish or, well, almost anything. The distrust was underscored by a deep throbbing sadness for all that had gone wrong, all that was still going wrong, much of it seemingly our own fault. Climate change was the biggest example. Close to home in Stehekin we'd seen shrinking glaciers and those increasingly frequent debilitating floods and bigger, hotter wildfires to boot. There were more insidious troubles, too. We'd seen a rash of cancer among our friends: young people, physically fit people, people who'd never touched a cigarette hacking themselves to death in hospital beds. You couldn't help but wonder about airborne pollutants trapped in fir needles released during forest fires or poisons from long-abandoned mountainside mines in our well water or polymers in the plastic bottles we drank snowmelt from. What had we done to our world? And what, if anything, could we do to make it right?

There were plenty of words to choose from—conservation, preservation, restoration—but most seemed to presume an idealized state, either one you cling to or one you try to recreate. If there were a word that might lead toward an answer, I thought, it'd have to be one that could hold contradiction, like nature itself. Mistakes and forgiveness. Creation and destruction and renewal. Reclamation. The word, I decided, came down to three concepts: to take back, to make right, and to make useful. The connotation was both moral and pragmatic, and sometimes the results were disastrous, but reclaiming seemed a nearly unstoppable human instinct.

One gray December—after yet another flood and the deaths of two close friends—Laurie and I drove a thousand miles south to Whiskeytown National Recreation Area west of Redding, California. Laurie had been hired to work on old apple trees planted by early settlers and barely hanging on. Over the years, the trees had been stunted by lack of sunlight, shaded by oaks and sequoias, strangled by blackberries. You get the picture. Nothing was going well for these trees until Laurie showed up. Never mind that at home she does exactly the same kind of work or that, except for this job, she'd be laid off for the season and we'd be skiing, her favorite pastime. She didn't need the money. She wanted to work on the trees because they needed it, but also because she wanted to honor the fact that someone worked like hell to plant them. You might think this had to do with what happened on our low ground, but it had more to do with her nature, and maybe human nature: she wanted to reclaim those trees.

Before she began, Laurie asked permission to burn as she went along. This is how she disposes of pruned limbs back home, and the warmth, in December, would be welcome. No way, the managers said. There's a midden. Rats? Laurie asked. No, no. An archaeological midden, a mound of obsidian chips several feet deep, the shavings from Indian tool makers, the Wintu, who lived at that spot along Clear Creek and in the surrounding Trinity Mountains, for twelve hundred years. Fire would melt the chips and destroy evidence of how they lived and worked. Rare evidence. Okay, then.

To be clear, Whiskeytown is not mainly about apple trees. Like most federally designated recreation areas, it's a reservoir, this one created in the early 1960s by an earthen dam. President Kennedy famously attended the dedication. Each morning after I dropped Laurie off to prune, watching her start a small chainsaw to cut through dormant vines, I stopped beside the human-made lake and gazed at the hills, lush and green even in December. Every single time I did, I saw other people standing on the shore looking out: young and old, well-dressed and shabby, a mother and daughter, a man in a business suit, all of them on their way from somewhere to somewhere else. They stood stone-still and stared, taking solace from the uncluttered view, the human-free landscape, all that water. The reclaimed lake was lovely, sure, but I was still troubled. Park brochures described how, on clear summer days, you could look down from a kayak and see the Old West storefronts of Main Street shimmering under the surface. The problem with reclaiming, I found myself thinking, is that it so often leads to displacing.

Back home in Stehekin, a river management plan had been in the works for months, a plan guaranteed to be unpopular. Stehekin consists of a patchwork of private property, about four hundred acres, tucked within the boundaries of Lake Chelan Recreation Area, which is managed by North Cascades National Park Service Complex. (There's a lake, yes, a natural one, though a dam raised its level by twenty feet in the 1920s.) The Park Service didn't arrive until the late 1960s, and the large-scale government presence isn't always welcome. The river plan would be a case in point.

A public meeting was scheduled. The gist was this: the Stehekin River needs more wiggle room, more freedom to wander, to crest its banks on occasion and seep outward democratically. No longer should dikes or dredging direct the course. At the meeting, National Park Service officials, many of them friends, arrived with PowerPoint presentations in hand, prepared to explain how these structures once built to protect us from floods now exacerbate the problem by sending the river pinballing toward the opposite shore and increasing erosion. They planned to describe a new series of small-scale structures and road relocations. But they got no chance. The room was super-packed with attendees spitting mad.

How did they not know of these plans? they cried. Plans they believed to be a subterfuge, a ruse to allow the feds to acquire private property from folks like my summer neighbors who'd sold out, to forcibly displace them.

I checked my watch, jiggled my feet, bowed my head to my chest. I did not look at our seething neighbors, did not glance over at Laurie sitting beside me, still in her work boots, did not risk eye contact with our silent baffled friends in ill-fitting Park Service uniforms—worn only on occasions like this—with their PowerPoints on permanent pause. I tried not to listen to the angry voices, only to the sounds underneath: the hum of laptop fans kicking on, the splash of wind-driven waves on the lake, Canadian geese honking in flight. Mostly I fought nausea. Razor-edged tension stretches through life in our idyllic little valley. Outsiders sometimes look at us with condescending mirth. ("What's the controversy this week?") How petty our battles seem, how transparently ideological. (Government is good! Government is bad!) From the inside, the struggles feel murkier—we own property, yes, we work for the Park Service, yes—and the strain feels visceral.

Who knows? I thought. The angry people might be right. The river management plan offered four alternatives that ranged from no action to degree variations on a theme: removal of structures and facilities from the channel migration zone. I read them several times, and I could not for the life of me make sense of them. I did know this much: A whole lot of private property in the valley, including our low ground, lay smack in the middle of the so-called channel migration zone, and the river was poised to reclaim it.

At the meeting, one man stood to say this:

"Remember this is Mother Nature. She might seem beautiful and docile, but really she's a bitch. You have to put her in her place, show her who's boss."

Chastise, he said, or maybe: Harness.

At Whiskeytown, while Laurie pruned, I set off in search of the story of who lived there before the dam and where they went. Not so much *what*. I could pretty much guess the fate of the fish and the forest, and while I did want to know about that, my sympathy right then lay mostly with the settlers in the drowned town and the Native people, the Wintu, before them.

A visitor center overlooked the placid lake, oil-dark on the surface. Around the shore low clouds fingered like smoke through dense green foliage toward a ridge brined with early wet snow. Inside, the place seemed much like a Park Service visitor center anywhere. Kids' books preached water conservation. Guidebooks described native plants. Coffee-table books featured photography of Indian basketry.

"What happened to the Wintu?" I asked the volunteer ranger, a middle-aged woman who told me she'd grown up in a nearby town and recently returned to the area.

"They moved on," she said. "They headed for the hills."

Three kiosk exhibits described the dam's construction and the local large mammal populations: deer, bear, cougar. The place felt like a kind of subsidized apology. But for what? I read descriptions of the dam construction, then reread them more closely. The idea was ambitious as hell—to dam the Trinity River, which flows west, and reverse the flow into the Sacramento River drainage to the east—and the details of construction were staggering: eight miles of tunnels 17.5 feet in diameter, 480,000 cubic yards of dirt to be excavated and relocated. The end result was piddling. Two powerhouses on the Whiskeytown reservoir generate a combined 300 megawatts today. (This was, I'd learn, peanuts by hydropower standards in the Pacific Northwest. None of the dams on the Columbia River generates less than a thousand megawatts.) And the reservoir provides irrigation, about 5,000 acres' worth. For this payoff, they'd reverse a river, flood a town, drown countless archaeological sites? I doubted it.

On Saturday, Laurie's day off, we met old friends and took a long walk beside the Sacramento River. The week had been rainy, but now the temperature registered balmy, shirt-sleeve warm. Dry yellow grass glistened in thin winter sun.

"But what's it really *for*?" I asked.

Our friend shrugged.

"Whiskeytown? That dam's for recreation."

"That's it. Recreation?"

"Of course," he said. "Who wouldn't want a lake in a valley that's over 100 degrees three months of the year?"

I was stunned. I'd convinced myself that people who reclaim things always have some decent purpose in mind, but that's the problem: the definition of a decent purpose is shifty. In a book about the national recreation area, I'd highlighted a quote from President Kennedy at the 1963 dedication.

"How great was the danger," he said, "that this great natural inheritance of ours given to us by nature, given to us by God, would be wiped away, the forests ruined, the streams destroyed, wasted for the people, water going to the sea unused."

John F. Kennedy. 1963. He meant wasted if there *wasn't* a dam.

In a photograph beside the quote, he feeds a mule deer.

I began a list of what gets reclaimed. Rivers. Swamps. Mines. Ball players. (Not to mention reclaimed identity—the empowering kind espoused in self-help books and the kind necessary when yours is stolen online.) Some examples were easily categorized. A new dam in China without fish ladders: bad. An aging Philadelphia Eagles receiver showing unexpected speed: good. Some examples edged toward deception: grass seed pressure-sprayed atop flattened former mountaintops to mitigate mining or new wetlands created in vacant lots to justify development elsewhere. But some stories were inspirational, very nearly triumphant, and the best seemed to be a kind of re-reclaiming. Taking back what had once been taken. Making right what had gone wrong. Redefining what useful might mean.

Even dams were coming down. A half-state away from my home in Washington State, two dams on the Elwha River flowing out of Olympic National Park were slated to be demolished. They'd be the first major dams in the country to be removed, and doing so would allow the return of historical runs of salmon, runs critical to the ecosystem and the local tribe, and if the hoopla surrounding the project was any indication, to our collective identity as half-decent stewards. The scheduled demolition was creating a kind of euphoria. And, of course, a ton of backlash.

My first-grade teacher used to tell us that saying "I'm sorry" meant you'd pounded a nail into a tree and now you've pulled it out. The hole is still there. Even as a kid I thought: well, then maybe it's best to leave the nail in. That seemed the argument against taking out the dams: that the hole would still be there, it would cost too much money, and maybe the entire deal would be for show. Over the next several months, I'd return over and over to the proverbial hole in the tree. So many ideologies hinge on the myth of a clean slate, the idea there's some undamaged state to preserve or restore. All better now! There isn't one. But here's the thing: the fact that there isn't one is no excuse. Our teacher, after all, wasn't telling us never to say sorry, only that we shouldn't use the power of apology as a cure-all or, worse, as permission to behave badly. It was, more than anything, an admonishment to proceed with care. We were only first graders, but we got it.

When I started telling friends about my interest in reclamation, everyone had a story. Did I know about High Line Park in New York City on a reclaimed elevated freight rail? How about Seattle's plan to reclaim wasted heat from data centers, the so-called Cloud, to power nearby neighborhoods? Reclaiming appeared everywhere, out of nowhere; it seemed to be, in some ways, the backdrop of our time. Nearly every major American city has a re-store where would-be remodelers can buy lumber and hardware salvaged from demolished buildings. Most watersheds have seen restoration, and some—the Hudson, the Cuyahoga— have been nothing short of miraculous. Even small-scale dam removal, it turns out, was nothing new. The nonprofit river advocacy group

American Rivers estimates that in the past century 925 dams have been removed from rivers.

Then there were Native Americans. If reclamation—at least the way it interested me—had to do with land and water, the original inhabitants were the ones with the most at stake. For the past fifty years, I'd learn, all across the country Indian tribes have been taking back what's been stolen from them: the Taos Pueblo in New Mexico, the Menominee in Wisconsin, the Passamaquoddy in Maine, the Colville in Washington. Even the Wintu, it turned out, did not all head for the hills as the volunteer ranger claimed, but still live and work and make headlines in North Central California, where they oppose raising Shasta Dam and have a plan to restore salmon in the McCloud River.

At the beginning, I didn't know any of this. I wouldn't until I left home.

So I did. Not long after our visit to Whiskeytown, I took a long solo trip— or more precisely a series of them—spurred by curiosity and hemmed by my own geography and finances. Over three years, I'd yo-yo up and down the west edge of the continent on either side of the long strip of mountains—Panamints, Sierras, Cascades—that have defined my adult life and alongside rivers that have, in literal ways, sustained me—the Feather, the Columbia, the Stehekin. I'd travel in an aging Buick along a zigzagging dot-to-dot route that loosely connects where I grew up in a desert suburb of Los Angeles to where I've landed in the North Cascades. I'd walk over sand dunes past lime-green mesquite and follow game trails among dormant oaks, watch steelhead through glass and befriend a single red fox. I'd talk to elders and activists, bureaucrats and lawyers and small-town mechanics. I'd tell everyone my three-part theory of reclaiming, and if their eyes occasionally glazed over at "taking back" and "making right"— weary perhaps of the eternal moral tug-of-war—by the time I got to "making useful," they had some things to say. And I tried to listen.

By chance and later with intention, I found myself immersed in the sagas of two small California tribes with big goals: the Timbisha Shoshone, who reclaimed their ancestral land in Furnace Creek in the center of Death Valley National Park more than a decade ago, and the Mountain Maidu, a federally unrecognized tribe in the Northern Sierras, who aimed to reclaim a sacred valley from a multinational utility company and planned to manage it using traditional ecological knowledge.

On the surface, these stories caught my attention because they dovetailed with my own experiences in Stehekin: the Timbisha had difficult dealings with the National Park Service, the Maidu worked their forested lands with chain saws and pruners—planting, thinning, harvesting—and held frequent community potlucks, much as we did. But there were deeper reasons as well. I'd written a book about my father's involvement in the early civil rights movement, and the heroes and she-roes I met doing the research, the everyday people who stood up to make a difference, had impressed me. I admired their courage, their fortitude, their unwavering faith. But like the Catholic faith of my childhood, their core beliefs lacked a deep connection with the earth: land, air, water, non-humans. That unspoken connection defined me. It bound me to Laurie. We met in the woods and still two decades later spend all our best time together outdoors: hiking dusty switchbacks through beetle-kill firs, skiing by the silent frozen river, tending our friends' neglected gardens, one after the next, in their absence. And it bound me to my neighbors, transcending even our most rancorous battles. Midwinter nearly every conversation in the post office centers on how many trumpeter swans have returned to the lake. (Thirty-seven one day, forty-three the next; everyone keeps count.) I claimed often that my interest in reclamation stemmed from intellectual curiosity, and joked half-earnestly that I mostly needed to get away from home—to think about any place else, to write about any place else—but underneath, always, lay something more. I wanted to explore that connection. I wanted to tell stories about people who try, in plain and practical ways, to take nature back, make it right, and make it useful. Even when ideas about how to do so shift infuriatingly.

Which brought me back to dams. I studied the history of dams and toured dams that are being refitted to make them *more* right, *more* useful, and finally settled in to learn the long saga of a major dam, the Condit dam on the White Salmon River, a tributary of the Columbia, coming down. What seemed at first the most straightforward story—explosives set the river free!—proved to be far more complicated. Dam removals expose human fallibility. Good earnest people once thought dams were a good idea; now good people wanted them to come down.

The stories melded over time into an uneasy triptych: the Timbisha Shoshone, the Maidu, the Condit removal. Along the way, I'd pick up threads of other stories, but these gripped me hardest, each story of its own accord, and the way their lessons intertwined and often enough contradicted one another.

If the ideas were bone-close, people brought them to life, especially three wise and savvy women, elders you might say, who stayed at their quests for decades. Pauline Esteves of the Timbisha Shoshone tribe. Beverly Ogle of the Mountain Maidu. Phyllis Clausen of Friends of the White Salmon River. At home now in Stehekin, I listen to their recorded voices—Pauline's fierce musical staccato, Beverly's meandering storyteller drawl, Phyllis's raspy precision—and hear their frequent laughter at themselves, at the knuckleheads they encountered, at the plain absurdity of it all. These women are charismatic, tenacious, and exceedingly humble. Ask them about their successes and they'll list their allies near and far, from relatives to bureaucrats to curious strangers and precious few deep-pocketed benefactors. They seem to see themselves as part of an interconnected whole, a human ecology. I've come to think of them, all of them, as "reclaimers"—the ones who reclaim.

In the end, there was one thing Laurie and I should have known about Whiskeytown but did not: there's poison oak everywhere. Those dormant vines she'd been sawing through? Yep. A month after our return, Laurie would require emergency room care and prednisone shots. It's a damned good thing, we'd agree, that she hadn't been allowed to burn. Meanwhile, we'd head home before Christmas, trade rain for snow, manzanita for Oregon grape, live oak for Douglas fir. We'd drive over the passes, show up at the funeral of yet another friend, and return to home where the river ran low. I'd walk a trail from the high ground to the low to pull skis out of the garage, where they hung from hooks we built in those early heady days, wedged behind a stovepipe that heated us when the garage doubled as a pool hall, and a fan that cooled us, and a shaggy shred of carpet Daisy used to climb to get above the fray. So much work, she seemed to think, what are you doing it for? The cat knew what we didn't. Now Daisy is gone, too. We hacked her grave in the frozen ground. The high ground, not the low.

The temptation is always there, isn't it? To give up, to give in. Admit that what we do, even with the very best intentions, is often futile and sometimes worse than that.

Until the need to make things right arises anew.

Our landless summer neighbors emailed in spring. They wanted to return to Stehekin for a visit and needed a place to camp, and our deserted low ground was the obvious choice. So Laurie and I started all over again: cleaning, watering, planting. We rigged up an outhouse with plywood scraps, a tarp, and an old pair of skis. We set up a campfire ring and set out some garbage cans. Our former neighbors, now neighbors again, set up a camper and a bug tent. We arrived for dinner with garden greens in paper towels and cut flowers in beer cans as afternoon sun backlit the berry brambles. The low ground, for the first time in a decade, felt right.

We knew it couldn't last.

Reclaimers

I

A Red-Lettered Sign

1

Homeland

Death Valley, California—March 2011

Asign along the roadside on California's Highway 190 caught my eye. The lettering was brilliant red and raised—Death Valley National Park—and an artist's rendition exaggerated the scenery that defined it: a red ridge in front of an orange ridge, in the distance blue sky and in the foreground white salt flats. Large timbers framed the sign with large iron corner braces, Old West style, atop a rock-faced base. None of that snagged my attention; it was the words that ran along the base.

Homeland of the Timbisha Shoshone.

I did a double take. Not that I was sleuthing. Not then, at least. I was on a short road trip with my mother, and I had no idea yet what the sign meant for the Timbisha Shoshone or how hard the fight had been. I knew only that the sign stood out. I'd worked in a couple of national parks and visited quite a few and never seen one like it.

Death Valley, at first, held no particular attraction. We'd been looking for a destination within driving distance of my mother's home and, except for one short drive-through for me, neither of us had ever been, so I flew from the rainy Northwest to sunny Southern California, arrived at midnight, and we hopped in the car at dawn. It'd be a six-hour trip, so we'd packed boxed juice and string cheese and granola bars, and as the traffic thinned on the interstate that connects Los Angeles to Las Vegas we talked about how Mom had, by then, survived five years with cancer. She still could not get over her luck, if that too-loose word could even apply.

She'd yanked herself back, by sheer force of will, from a nursing home bed to the passenger seat of a Camry cruising the freeway past the rough suburb where she taught Spanish at the community college before she retired, and farther on, through the spooky two-lane bottleneck in Adelante, lined with billboards for bankruptcy lawyers and strip clubs, through the flat high desert expanse where power lines bisect the sky and Joshua trees stand with bent-branch limbs, and onto 395. We passed the snowcapped Sierras to the west and the China Lake Naval Weapons Station, the navy's largest landholding, over a million acres, just as close to the east.

We talked politics and gossiped about relatives and always she returned to the singular truth.

"I didn't die," she said. "I thought I would die."

We arrived in Owens Valley, the high dry valley a hundred miles west of Furnace Creek, too early in the afternoon to hunker in a motel room, but too late to venture into the park, so we decided to spend the afternoon at Manzanar, the site of the World War II Japanese internment camp. A friend of my mother's had visited Manzanar and deemed it the best museum she'd ever visited. So we treated it with travelers' nonchalance: why not? Still, the series of ironic holiday destinations, however unintentional, was lost on neither of us: Death Valley for someone who'd narrowly evaded death, an internment camp for a woman who'd so recently been confined to bed.

At Manzanar the wind blew hard and icy-cold and mist swirled behind the stonework entryway, an eerie testament to the industriousness of the prisoners. The setting, smack against the steep granite face of the Sierras, seemed inhospitable and gorgeous at once, the kind of place where you'd want to live but might be afraid to. Which pretty much sums up the history. We walked into the visitor center and saw right away what my mother's friend meant. The place is ambitious, huge in scale and design and also in its message, which is determinedly broad. Large wall-mounted displays tell the history of Owens Valley in succession. Not starting with the Japanese, but going back through story after story of displacement. Back, back, back. Mom walked slowly, caneless but unsteady, so we stopped to read each display completely.

First came the indigenous people.

The Paiute, who inhabited Owens Valley for 1,500 years, hunted deer and elk and bighorn sheep and tended willows for baskets and diverted local streams to irrigate yellow nutgrass and wild hyacinth. Wild hyacinth!

Then came the whites.

Beginning in the 1830s, mountain men, then miners showed up, followed by ranchers who let their cattle roam indiscriminately. The cattle decimated the nutgrass and hyacinth and outcompeted the deer and elk and bighorn sheep for what was left to browse, causing wild animals to die of starvation and nudging the Indians toward a similar fate. The situation grew dire in 1862 when autumn floods charged down from a too-early snow in the Sierras, killing off the remaining deer and elk and drowning the remaining fields. So, the Paiutes started killing cattle for food—it seemed only fair—and the ranchers didn't like it one bit.

Then came the army.

Cavalrymen moved in exactly like they'd do in the Hollywood westerns that'd be filmed in Owens Valley a half-century later and chased the valley-dwelling Paiutes up the mountains, and the Paiutes sneaked back down, over and over again. The game of cat and mouse infuriated the soldiers who, in 1863, murdered thirty-five Indians in what became known as the Keyesville Massacre. (Archaeologists still pluck bullets and musket balls and uniform buttons from the alkali flats where the murders took place.) In the same year, while the Civil War raged in the East, the army herded up all the Indians it could find, more than nine hundred in all, and walked them south to reservations in a little-known California version of the Trail of Tears.

Then came a thriving fruit industry.

By the turn of the century, the Owens River irrigated five thousand acres of apples, pear, and peach trees. Even when the lake level began to drop as a result, no one seemed too concerned. Watercolor renderings of the orchards adorn postcards in the Manzanar gift shop: pink-blossomed rows against a backdrop of granite peaks rising. The valley is green, the snow white, the sky blue, the scene bucolic. The small town with a tree-lined street and a general store called itself Manzanar, from *manzana*, Spanish for apples.

"Maybe Manzanar means to apple?" my mother said.

She pondered the conjugation while I pondered the displacements. Which only got worse.

Then came the water wars.

In 1913, Los Angeles mayor Fred Eaton and his hand-picked water superintendent, William Mulholland, famously constructed an aqueduct to transport water from the Owens River to the city. They bought up land for well below its value and claimed they'd use the water strictly for urban domestic purposes but instead used it to irrigate the arid San Fernando Valley. Liars and cheats, it's fair to say. The residents of Owens Valley got so furious they dynamited a section of the aqueduct. All for naught. Los Angeles flourished. Owens Lake turned into an alkali flat.

Then came the Japanese.

This is the story people come to Manzanar to hear, to honor, to bear witness to, and the details are familiar but haunting. The Japanese were rounded up during World War II, stripped of land and dignity, and transported to cold inland places, safely away from the Pacific Ocean. Places like Manzanar. To be imprisoned, scholars now insist, not held. At concentration camps, they say, not internment camps. The government determined they were enemies, but that was not the whole of it. Only the Japanese were imprisoned. Not the Germans. (Mom is half German.) Not the Italians. (I am one-quarter Italian.) Our relatives were lucky, but it's luck that's tainted by privilege and prejudice and earned by violence. We walked though the visitor center and pictured ten thousand people in one square mile and read the loyalty oaths that internees were required to sign. We watched a film in a plush-seat theater that showed the gardens the prisoners grew, complete with arched stone bridges, and the furniture they built, the children they raised, the May Day parades they held. The message of the film was hard to parse: resilience perhaps, how to make the most of it, how they were not whiners.

I was unnerved by the history, which was precisely the effect the museum designers had in mind, but I was also struck by the government's willingness to dedicate a multimillion-dollar visitor center, nuanced and researched, to a mistake. A big one. Later I'd learn that it took activists decades to force the government to take notice, that it was not exactly a spontaneous gesture of penitence. But in the moment, I felt a small measure of pride.

"See," I said, "at least our country admits the truth about what's gone wrong."

My mother shook her head vehemently and eyed me like I was a simpleton or a traitor.

"It's not enough," she said.

We circled toward a central display which conjured other eras, not so distant, when patriotism trumped principle: Kent State, 9/11, immigration debates. I tried to steer Mom to another, smaller film screen where you could watch Ronald Reagan apologize on behalf of all Americans and dedicate the site we stood on, but she would have none of it. She marched directly to the guest book at the door to scrawl in all caps: NEVER AGAIN.

Morning. The snowy Sierras receded in our rearview mirror, the Panamints rose ahead, and we drove toward the quiet west entrance of the park, the only car on the road for miles. The landscape spread broad but not empty, startling but not gaudy like the canyon country of Arizona and Utah: not gutted and gullied by water, not temporary as sandstone. The Panamints, stark desert mountains, are big and broad, and the colors are subtle, and the plant life is modest: rabbitbrush and sage, tumbleweeds in the making. We'd started in Lone Pine at 4,000 feet among leafless poplars and single-wide trailers and chain motels. Joshua trees didn't appear until we gained another thousand feet, their spike-like tufts halfway between cacti and palms. Pinyon pines colonized mountainsides higher yet, bushier and green. We drove in comfortable silence, Mom and I, climbing ever higher as the white highway lines on either side of us converged toward the horizon, ridges beyond ridges beyond ridges, toward a sky streaked with thin cirrus clouds.

That's when we passed the sign: Homeland.

"What do you think that means?" I asked my mother.

"Just what it says."

Justice, to my mother, is matter-of-fact, both a prerogative and a given. If the place belongs to the Indians, it does. But I knew the National Park Service better than that. I agreed with her, of course, about what was right, but not the inevitability of it. That sign did not appear on its own. I wanted to know how this came to be, these raised red letters on a signboard, how you might carve, or re-carve, a homeland out of a place that welcomes nearly a million tourists annually. The highway climbed to a narrow pass, and we began the steep curvy descent into the valley below.

It's an understatement, I suppose, to call the geography of Death Valley extreme. The double set of mountains to the west—the 14,000-foot-high Sierras, the 11,000-foot-high Panamints—block clouds drifting in from the ocean, keeping annual rainfall on the valley floor at less than three inches. Add the 9,000-foot-high Armargosas to the east, and the relief in Death Valley is more dramatic than in the Cascades, where, besides volcanoes, the mountains aren't as high, and more dramatic than the Rockies, too, where you start out higher. The mountains recirculate hot air like a convection oven, causing famously record-breaking temperatures: 134 degrees in July 2013. Tourists fry eggs on the pavement. Others organize ultramarathons in midsummer to prove their mettle. It's out of the way—a three-hour drive from Vegas, six from Los Angeles—and it's on the way to nowhere. Once, between seasonal jobs, Laurie and I had driven a Toyota Corolla loaded with all our earthly possessions into Death Valley from the east and out to the west, coaxing four cylinders up the same 9 percent grade Mom and I just descended as a scenic detour on the way from Arizona to Oregon. We wrecked the transmission with the strain. Too much work. And that seemed pretty much the story of Death Valley, at least from the white perspective. Hard work to get here, hard work to get out, and while you're here: survival. The valley floor is flat, no hummocks or gullies, no yellow-tipped rabbitbrush or sage, no boulders, only shoebox-sized rocks strewn over sand and salt. Your gaze can sweep hundreds of miles unimpeded. Germans especially flock to the place for just this reason, to see the kind of uninhabited expanse unthinkable in Europe. As Mom and I approached Stovepipe Wells, I tried to gauge my own discomfited reaction to the landscape. The place was raw, oppressive, expansive. I felt vulnerable.

Soon we began to see tourists everywhere: in campgrounds crammed tight with RVs of every size, some longer and wider than a Greyhound bus with satellite dishes sprouted on the sides, on bicycles on the shoulderless side of the road, and in the distance hiking over sand dunes that rose with a sculptor's perfection; there was something like seduction in the swoop and shadow. The view from the top, I thought, would be awesome. But this trip was not for hiking.

Mom and I stopped at a kiosk, where she was disappointed to find no one collecting fees—off-season perhaps—since she'd love to show off her lifetime senior pass. We grabbed a copy of the official park brochure, unfolded it open, and saw a sight more startling than the scenery or even the entrance sign. A shaded box: Timbisha Shoshone Homeland. Not the kind of shading that means: here's a place to camp for the night, or get good views here. This appeared to be the kind of shading that means another jurisdiction: a military installation, say, or a private inholding, maybe state or county land.

The brochure told the story in brief. The Timbisha Shoshone Indians trace their ancestry in Death Valley back more than ten thousand years to the end of the last ice age, but they did not hold official title to any of their vast ancestral homeland until the year 2000, when the United States returned three hundred acres of it to them "to live on in perpetuity." The map showed the three hundred shaded acres not half a mile from Furnace Creek, the very center of the park, with a golf course, swimming pools, and a famous $400/night inn. Later I'd piece together an extended version of the story.

The Timbisha were a loose band related by language and culture to the Western Shoshone. Historians estimate as many as fifteen hundred of them lived in Furnace Creek beside natural springs in the eighteenth century; they hunted deer and bighorn sheep, even reptiles; they tended mesquite, pounding the beans into a paste, and pinyon trees, harvesting the rich nuts from the higher mountain slopes in summer and saving them through the winter.

In the late 1800s, Pacific Borax Company bought land in Death Valley and began to mine the white salt-like ore, the uses of which are enumerated in the popular Borax Museum at Furnace Creek: laundry soap, pesticide, fire retardant, flux, and enamel glaze. Images of Death Valley often feature the twenty-mule teams that first hauled the ore to railheads. (Twenty mules! No wonder the Corolla couldn't do the job.) When the cost of transporting the ore made competition too stiff, the company realized that a richer treasure lay in scenery and the people who'd flock to see it. Timbisha laborers lived in brush shelters as they built the swimming pools and the golf course and the famous inn. The harder they worked, the more land got developed, and the farther the company moved them from the natural springs.

Then came the National Park Service. Indian villages, it turns out, were not uncommon in national parks. Some, with teepees and drumming and face-painted Native performers, were considered attractions. But it was never an easy truce, and though few Americans know the history—I didn't until I started reading about the Timbisha—the whole bargain usually turned sour for the Indians. In Mesa Verde, park officials swindled the Utes out of cliff-dwelling sites by trading them land they already owned. In Pipe Springs, Mormon managers co-opted water rights from Paiutes. In Yosemite, the Indian Village was burned down repeatedly, most recently in the 1960s. Indians were an embarrassment to the Park Service because they lived poorly, because they lived differently, and mostly because they lived where they lived. So when Herbert Hoover signed legislation to create Death Valley National Monument in 1933, it meant trouble. But the Timbisha weren't going anywhere. When, in the 1950s, the Park Service tore down some of the original adobe dwellings while the Timbisha residents were in the mountains for the summer, the Indians returned, moved into mobile trailers, and stayed year-round. When, in the 1960s, the Park Service charged rent to try to chase them out, the Timbisha refused to pay. Furnace Creek was their home.

Approaching Furnace Creek, Mom and I could see the palms and mesquites oasis-like on the horizon. The place was far greener than Stovepipe Wells, more developed, and even busier. Besides the high-end accoutrements, the small village featured a wooden-front strip mall with gift shops, a bar, a motel, soda machines, and shaded seating. We headed to the café, where we ate tuna melts and drank iced tea and wrote postcards to my nieces and nephews, then we walked across a green watered lawn to mail them at the small post office. We were eager to see the visitor center, and a little disappointed to find it temporarily housed in a trailer while a newer, bigger one was being constructed. We walked a makeshift ramp to the door—Mom was still avoiding stairs where possible—and stepped inside to look at maps and photos, to page through books, plenty of them, on wildlife to see and hikes to take, on the history of the Borax Company and, again, always, the twenty-mule teams. But not one on the Timbisha Shoshone. I thought to ask the fellow behind the desk—a boisterous ranger in a crisp green tie and the requisite flat hat, who announced to everyone who entered that he was from Oklahoma—about the land reclamation, but the line was long, and Mom was tired, and I suspected he wouldn't know much.

We returned to the car in the crowded lot, and Mom fell asleep in the passenger seat. As I drove, I pondered the idea of the Homeland Act, wondering who could make such a thing happen. In every article I'd later find, one name appeared over and over: Pauline Esteves.

Esteves, from what I could gather, was an octogenarian activist, an elder and tribal leader who, according to several patchwork biographies, possessed hard-won authority. Born at Furnace Creek in 1925, the daughter of a Basque father and a Timbisha mother, she was old enough to remember the day in 1936 when park rangers forced her family to move from the springs to Indian Village. She lived her whole life in Indian Village and even worked for the Park Service in the 1970s, when, according to one story, she one day confronted a group of visitors who were standing around discussing energy policy, a hot topic at the time.

Well, Esteves explained to the tourists, you could say her people, the Timbisha Shoshone, were the best conservationists in Death Valley since their homes had no electricity. No electricity, no water rights, no insulation. In fact, the United States government more or less considered them squatters on their own land. The park superintendent called her in directly and threatened to fire her if she did not stop saying such things. But she never did.

Instead, she attended meetings and penned letters and filed lawsuits. She marched into the Nevada Test Site to protest nuclear weapons testing on former Timbisha land. She traveled to Germany and Hungary to speak on behalf of the tribe in solidarity with other indigenous people. When the time came, she served as the lead negotiator for the tribe and penned a preface to the *Draft Secretarial Report to Congress* on the Homeland Act, an oft-cited and oft-reprinted document. In it, she recounts injustices and concludes, "We are part of our Homeland and it is part of us. We are people of the land. We don't break away from what is part of us." Her plain-spoken moral clarity, her righteous tone, and the message itself—we're connected, we belong—moved me. If the idea of returning to Death Valley and trying to meet Pauline Esteves and hear her story firsthand had not already lodged hard in me, it did now. As did one last description, from a profile in the *New Yorker* by Ian Frazier. Esteves, he said, was a "dour and heavyset woman" who claimed that people who wrote about her "got almost everything wrong."

That posed a problem. Much as I might like to talk to Pauline Esteves, I could very easily get everything wrong. I knew about the dangers of appropriation; some stories don't belong to outsiders. Still, I was intrigued.

As we drove through the park in the hot midday sun I looked to my mother, the keeper of moral hard lines, still asleep in the passenger seat. She lost her hair from the chemotherapy and it had grown back a soft downy white. If there were a guest book at an exhibit about the Timbisha Homeland Act, what would she write? Way to go! Or: Too little too late!

Not far past the Badlands, elevation 242 feet below sea level, where tourists ventured out into the fractured salt flats, octagon-shaped with white crust peeling like skin after a sunburn, Mom awoke with a start. The Panamints rose to the west, the Armagosas to the east. She blinked in amazement, remembering how far we'd come.

"Look where we are," she said.

It was the time of year for wildflowers, but few were out. Still, we wanted to at least pull over and see what we could see. On the shoulder of the road, we bent in unison to see wispy purple flowers, nearly unnoticeable. Before the day was through, we'd watch a coyote and a raven cavort in a culvert. Signs would lead us to an old mining cache, rusty discarded tools strewn in the desert, and the highway would take us back to the six-lane interstate and a Burger King meal and the crush of people that is, for my mother, and maybe for me, too, our homeland. That night, while my mother slept, I'd discover a photograph of Pauline Esteves on the official Park Service website and study her profile in the flickering computer screen light: deeply lined and regal, slightly bemused. Not the least bit dour.

Meanwhile, on the shoulder of the road, we stepped back into the car as the sunlight faded into swaths of gray, and my mother turned to me. She'd wanted to see Death Valley before she died.

"It's better," she said, "than I ever imagined it."

2

Willkommen

Rocky Reach Dam, Columbia River, Washington—June 2011

The dam tour guide, José, young and affable, solid and muscular like a former high school wrestler, stood directly across from three picture windows in the basement fish ladder viewing room and worked like hell to keep our attention fixed on a painted mural that illustrated the life cycle of the salmon, but it wasn't going well.

"Look, there's one!" one woman cried.

We swiveled our heads in unison to see a silver fish flash in dark murky water.

"Steelhead," José said.

He waited a beat then tried to return to his tale: how salmon start in the small streams, travel to the ocean, then return.

We only half listened.

Partly because we knew the story already. Or many of us did. I had to make the tour reservation in advance online. For how many? the online form asked. One, I checked. Just me. But then Laurie wanted to come, and our friend Shari—a summer neighbor and a retired schoolteacher, recently widowed, whose land flooded each time ours did—wanted to come, and Shari asked if she could bring a group of friends, many of them former teachers as well. They'd be making the usual tourist stops, including lunch in nearby Leavenworth, a faux German tourist destination where storefronts are Bavarian by enforcement, and the streets are crowded with plenty of lederhosen and sausage and beer. A dam tour? Why not? There's something old-fashioned and patriotic about touring the local power plant on a warm summer day. By the time we arrived at Rocky Reach dam, we were eight women, most but not all long-term residents of the Pacific Northwest. So we knew about salmon.

Salmon are the symbol of the region, the crux of the fiercest debates and the most expensive lawsuits of the past fifty years; their Northwest habitat dwindles even as they remain ubiquitous on Northwest postcards and products and on the tables of all fine Northwest restaurant tables. We knew plenty about them, yes, but we didn't get to see them like this, up close and personal, very often.

We watched rapt until the steelhead zipped away, heading up the fish ladder—92 feet in elevation over sixteen long steps—then onward upriver. It was a mesmerizing sight and one that filled me with regret for not visiting the previous fall when there'd been a record sockeye run. While sockeye salmon aren't among the endangered subspecies on this river section—the official listings are site specific—the record run had still come as a surprise. Some days a thousand salmon swam up the fish ladder at Rocky Reach every hour. Every *hour*. I was sorry I'd missed it.

José drew our attention back toward the mural, all pastels and arrows like an illustration in a middle school textbook, to explain how of five thousand eggs only six to eight will survive to make the trip back home and how, despite what you may have heard, the way they do so is no mystery, not really: they smell their way. Their sense of smell is one hundred times better than a dog's. Still, the odds are against survival.

"The dams are not the problem," José insisted.

Commercial fishermen are, he said. Or the aggressive non-native northern pikeminnow is. There's logging which causes siltation and overheating of the spawning streams; there's development and the misguided river management techniques of yesteryear that dredged away log jams, critical salmon habitat. His little mini-lecture seemed like a postmodern public relations version of reclaiming: to take back the story, to deflect blame, to spin the facts. It would have been more frustrating if not for the fact that everyone in the group, probably everyone in America, knew exactly how to deal with spin: we ignored it.

"Look, there's another one!" Shari cried, and we turned to watch another muscular fish, the length and width of my calf, loiter beside the glass, tail undulating.

José moved on to fish mechanics: the back rudder for slow turns, the front rudder for a brake, the dorsal fin for balance, and the adipose fin that's cut off hatchery fish, the telltale for fishermen who can keep those but not the wild ones. Shari knew all about that, since her husband had been an avid fisherman. But this was news to me.

When we had no more questions, we climbed the stairs and stepped out into the sun and the delightful shock of early summer: the sky blue with puffy clouds, the flowers in bloom, and the spillways wide open. It had been an excellent snow year in the Cascades, so news reports told of water being spilled past dams from here to the Pacific. Mist billowed high over the concrete, and all that water spraying on a sunny day makes for as much giddy childlike glee as open fire hydrants on a city street.

Along the Columbia River, Rocky Reach Dam is a third of the way from Canada to the Pacific in the heart of orchard country; nearby Wenatchee claims to be the nation's apple capital. The Columbia this far up is not as dramatic as down by Oregon; it doesn't even merit the label "gorge." The floodplain is wider due to ice age floods, the residue of ancient Lake Missoula. Modern-day Lake Entiat, the lake created by the dam, is a kind of hybrid reservoir, more flattened-out current than lake. Some people, even locals, don't realize this is the mighty Columbia. There's no interstate, no major city, no waterfalls. Except where it's irrigated, there's no trademark Northwest green. I gazed upriver, trying again to picture the river as it was before the dams. I couldn't come close.

To the south, grain crops grow on the flats of a plateau as far as you can see; towns like Waterville and Mansfield look as though they could be in North Dakota. To the north, the snow-clad North Cascades, the source of all this tumult, stretch undeveloped for millions of acres. The peaks are close but, from here, not quite visible.

Up there, in those water-rich mountains, is where I live. The Stehekin River drainage is the longest continuous U-shaped valley in the Lower 48, and it's fed by more than a hundred small glaciers and heavy winter snowfall to boot. In summer, you can stand on switchbacks near the Cascades crest and see the path an ancient ice sheet carved, a vast forested bathtub trough that stretches as far as you can see. You can gaze out to see talus and brush and cedar and fir, blue glacial lakes and remnant patches of snow, but all you will hear is water. Running, pouring, charging, trickling.

If you follow the river twenty miles or so down from the crest, you come to Company Creek, a side creek that's home to the Stehekin Power Plant. Built in the 1960s amidst considerable controversy—people liked living off the grid and feared change, too—the plant diverts water from the creek into a three-foot-diameter steel pipe which carries it to the powerhouse, where a needle valve aims it at a Pelton wheel that powers our lights and refrigerators and televisions and computers. As long as the operator keeps the intake clear of leaves and rocks and ice, as long as the overhead lines aren't knocked out by falling trees, hydropower is ready and available. And cheap.

Of course it's subsidized. There's no way one hundred residents could pay enough for it. Chelan County PUD, the same utility district that runs Rocky Reach Dam, pays for the operator and the upkeep. So, we're off the grid physically; we don't receive power from outside sources, nor do we give it. Still, even here in the land of self-sufficiency, where a large faction of neighbors rages against socialism and bucks big government, we benefit from public power. Truth is, neither the use of the water nor the subsidy has ever seemed to me anything but good.

If you follow the river farther to where it flows into Lake Chelan and a couple miles more, you reach Flick Creek House. There, beyond the reach of even the Stehekin grid, photographers Mike and Nancy Barnhart used to use a generator to power their self-built cabin, but the generator was noisy and the gas was expensive and they had water rights to nearby Flick Creek, so why not try mini-hydro? Mike designed the system himself. I'd helped him at times over the years—hauling lumber for a siltation catch basin, clearing downed trees along the intake trail, gluing together sections of two-inch PVC pipe—and I'd been wowed, every time, by the plain elegance. The diverted water drops 250 vertical feet, through the PVC, from a small dammed pool no larger than a church fountain to create 120 pounds of pressure that shoots through two tiny nozzles in a board-and-batten shed near the cabin to turn a six-inch waterwheel attached to a heavy-duty alternator no larger than what's on an eighteen-wheeler. Voila! There are no anadromous fish in Flick Creek. The water returns to the creek and then to the lake. The entire DIY system is clean, efficient, non-damaging, ingenious.

Next comes the lake. On a map, Lake Chelan, fifty-five miles long, narrow and fjord-like, fingering toward Canada, looks like a reservoir. It's not—it's a natural lake—but it's also dammed. The dam is small by Columbia River standards, but despite being built in 1903—the same era as the two slated for demolition on the Elwha—the Lake Chelan Hydroelectric Project creates 59 megawatts, nearly three times as much as those dams, and has been certified as "green" by the Low Impact Hydropower Institute. More good hydropower.

Below the Lake Chelan dam, water pours down a steep narrow canyon through the small town of Chelan Falls (the "green" designation stems, in part, from the fact that fish never could make it up the former falls from the river to the lake) and spills into the Columbia itself. That's where the trouble begins.

Sixteen dams were built on the Columbia River in the twentieth century, and each seemed to wreak more havoc than the last. In 1933 the first of them, Rock Island Dam not far downstream from Wenatchee, drowned some 350 petroglyphs. In 1942 Grand Coulee Dam blocked salmon traffic from over fourteen hundred river miles. Engineers for this darling of the New Deal failed to install fish ladders to save costs, even though the technology was ready and available and had, in fact, been in use at Bonneville dam for over a decade. In 1957, despite failed negotiations with and loud protests from Yakama, Warm Springs, Umatilla, and Nez Perce leaders, the Dalles Dam destroyed Celilo Falls, the heart of Indian fishing on the river, and the village of Celilo itself, the longest continuously inhabited settlement in North America. And so it went.

Reclaimers

I'd spent weeks reading about the dams before arriving at Rocky Reach for the tour. With my back against a cedar tree, I'd sit beside the Stehekin River, the cacophony of charging water as soundtrack as I read memoirs of Colville Indians who remembered thousands of salmon leaping upriver at Kettle Falls and the shock when Grand Coulee smoothed it sterile. I read histories of the Entiat and Chelan Indians who assimilated rather than get annihilated, and I tried to imagine what the right choice would be in that situation with a bleak future writ large before your eyes. Top hat and long coat or war paint and a celluloid future? I could only read in short spurts before I'd replace a bookmark and stand to toss rocks or douse my sandaled feet in the icy churn.

I told myself it was because the information was dense—all those dams, all those dates—but I knew it wasn't true. My theory about the earnest good intentions that drive reclaimers was proving to be complicated, if not plain wrong. What's worse, I felt personally implicated. What the miners did in Death Valley, you can attribute to a few roughneck single men, but the blame for what happened on the Columbia falls on all of us, the government and the true believers and Woody Guthrie singing "Roll On Columbia" while backwater filled sacred sites and salmon smelled their way into walls of cement.

Our tour group grew more animated out in the sun, snapping pictures, telling stories, yelling to be heard over the sound of the charging river below. Now we followed José into the powerhouse, the shortest and most traditional part of the tour. Below us we could see, through safety glass installed after 9/11, the eleven immense generators, cylindrical and half-submerged, with their tops brightly painted like the caps of fire hydrants. We could hear the roar, airport loud and white noise steady, of the turbines spinning at unfathomable speed. A display with a hand crank let us experience how much effort it takes to light a single bulb. The answer is: a lot.

Each of the women took a turn spinning, the first few trying gamely one-handed to no avail, then each woman trying harder, and laughing. Still nothing. With a two-handed grip and a grimace, I gave it my all. A flicker showed briefly, and faded. Laurie stepped up and kept the bulb shining for a solid fifteen seconds or so, a feat that caused her to have a sore back for days.

José, for his part, refused to take a turn.

"I've learned that lesson," he said with a grin.

Rocky Reach belongs to a utilitarian era of architecture—construction began in 1956 and was completed in 1961—that allowed for none of the grandeur or grace of the Depression-era dams. There's something distinctly Eisenhower administration about the place. The dam itself, wide and flat, is understated and practical; the visitor center is all sleek lines and glass and steel, something from *I Dream of Jeannie* or *Love American Style*. If Rocky Reach Dam is impressive, in other words, it's only because it's big, like a workaday offensive lineman. It's there to get the job done.

And a big job it is. Rocky Reach puts out 1,300 megawatts of power, enough to power over a million homes. Hoover Dam, by comparison, for all its glamour, puts out only 2,000. Grand Coulee, the pride of the Columbia, puts out 7,000.

"What's the biggest dam in the world?" José asked.

None of us knew.

"Three Gorges in China. Twenty-one thousand megawatts. Displaced 1.5 million people."

He went on to explain more about the problems. No concrete in the aft-bay to prevent erosion, and no fish ladder at all.

"And you've heard about the Elwha?"

The dam removals were three months off and already dominated the news. The 105-foot Elwha Dam and the 210-foot Glines Canyon Dam, built in the early twentieth century, together generated only an average of 19 megawatts. And, like Three Gorges and Grand Coulee, they had no fish ladders at all. No way for endangered salmon to travel from the Strait of Juan de Fuca into Olympic National Park. The first President Bush signed the Elwha Restoration Act in 1992, and it had taken two decades to iron out the details, to balance the demands of stakeholders including tribes and environmental groups and the National Park Service, and mostly, to secure funding. Now funding was forthcoming: Obama administration stimulus money, lots of it, and lots of press too.

So, yes, we'd heard.

I'd even planned to attend the breaching, to see history in the making, or the unmaking in this case, until I talked with a poet friend who lived near Port Angeles, the town closest to the dams. We sat on a dock beside yet another dam-built lake—Diablo Lake on the Skagit River—where together we were teaching a nature writing class, and after a dunk in the frigid water, we reminisced about the old days, how when we'd arrived in the Pacific Northwest it was all about wet leather boots and wool socks by the campfire. We'd both worked for the Park Service, me in the North Cascades and him in the Olympics, and so naturally talk turned to the Elwha. When I told him I planned to drive eight hours for the big event, he laughed. He'd been involved as an activist for twenty years, he said, and couldn't get a ticket. Of course, it'd still be fun to be in town, he said. There'd be a band at the local high school, there'd be a parade.

"A parade?" I asked.

He chuckled a little, and together we stared out at the dam and listened to the crackle of power lines overhead.

I decided not to make the trip.

Back at Rocky Reach José led us toward a small-scale model of the turbines and raised his voice to be heard over the roar of the real ones below. He described hydropower in shorthand: how water spins the turbine, which turns the rotor, which holds electromagnets, which generate current in the copper coils, which moves through the transformers and, when phases are synced, makes electricity instantly available all over the West as part of the grid. The process is remarkably efficient, but to make it even more so, the eleven turbines were replaced at the end of the 1990s. While they were at it, engineers redesigned them to increase the survival rate of juvenile fish heading for the sea. For forty years, those fish have had to dive ninety feet deep, following the current, and shoot through huge steel fins spinning like a superfast revolving door. With the redesign, they'd have a 93 percent chance of survival.

"That's pretty good," José said. "But not good enough."

Here at last came the reason I'd become fascinated with this particular dam. José pointed out the window at a large concrete tube snaking around the powerhouse and past the spillways and along the far bank to where it suddenly stopped and water poured out the end like from an oversized spigot. The juvenile fish bypass. I'd noticed it each time I'd driven by for months. From the highway it looked like a waterslide. From inside the powerhouse, it looked bigger, more industrial. I could not imagine how it worked.

Say you are a yearling salmon or steelhead, maybe ten inches long, or even a sub-yearling, the size of a goldfish, and you're heading out to sea, swimming downstream on the Columbia. You get to Rocky Reach Dam and you have two choices. You can take the route your ancestors have taken since they first faced the dam in the 1960s: Dive deep with the current, and swim on through one of eleven turbines turning like a superfast revolving door. Choose that route and you have a much greater chance of survival. Not bad. But nowadays you've got another option. You can ease into the surface flow of 6,000 cubic feet per second artificially created just for you. The flow will seduce you into the giant nine-foot tunnel in which you'll turn backwards and coast for five or seven minutes. Then you'll drop into the current well below the dam, in the fastest deepest water, and continue on your merry way.

Your chance of survival is about 99.9 percent.

"Ninety nine point nine," José boasted.

Chelan PUD completed the $120 million structure in 2003. I'd assumed it did so because a judge told it to or because activists forced its hand. Which is true on the grand scale. As various salmon runs have been listed under the Endangered Species Act, power companies have been required to spill more water at certain times of year to create better conditions for the fish. And more water spilled means less water available for power generation, which means less revenue. Even if no such requirement had yet been made at Rocky Reach, it was expected to come someday. This was a kind of pre-emptive mitigation, a dollar-and-cents decision, as much as an act of good faith.

"Maybe they did it so there'd be no lag time between when they'd be required to spill and when they came up with a solution?" I suggested.

José smiled and shrugged.

"Maybe we did it so fish will live," he said.

He smiled and led us up one more flight of stairs to the top floor, where an impressive regional history museum is housed.

We were greeted by a hand-painted banner. *Willkommen.* Welcome. It took a few minutes to realize the message was intended not for us, but for the salmon. A large display of third graders' paintings depicted the salmon's life cycle with more color and exuberance than the outmoded murals in the basement. The third graders were from nearby Leavenworth, the faux-Bavarian town—hence the bilingual greeting—and somehow that seemed fitting. In the 1960s Leavenworth was just another dying logging town when someone worked up the German-themed scheme. To some locals it must have seemed ridiculous. A Hail Mary pass, a gamble. But the amazing part of the story is how well it worked. Leavenworth thrives like few small Washington towns. On summer days, bumper-to-bumper traffic slows to let kids with waffle cones jaywalk while camera-slinging international tourists, some rumored to be guest workers at Microsoft, de-board tour buses to admire chainsaw carvings in the park. The place is not really German, but pretending to be saved it.

Which made me wonder about Rocky Reach. I couldn't shake the sense of irony in all the focus on the fish. Isn't it a little absurd to post "Welcome" signs right at the structure that, without all this engineering, would stop salmon cold? On the other hand, would it be better to ignore the fish? The dam is not really about the fish, not even close, but pretending it is might really save some of them.

The tour ended in a museum hallway lined disconcertingly with portraits of Indians from the area, several of them Nez Perce who fought the government so valiantly and lost.

"Any more questions?"

"About the record sockeye run last year. Was the juvenile bypass responsible?" I asked.

José remained equivocal. The scientists aren't sure, he said. Warmer oceans probably played a role, for better or worse, as well as fewer predators.

"But it sure didn't hurt," he said.

José was not saying that there's no such thing as bad dams—he had cited them in fact—he was saying only that this dam was not one of them, that they are trying to make things right. There'd be no parade about this, no rock band at the local high school. Reclaiming, I realized, is easier to celebrate when it's a total do-over like baptism—born again!—rather than a slow process marked by single-digit percentage improvements. I stood staring down at the generators, whirring loudly, and out the windows at the massive concrete fish bypass suspended over the water. You had to admit: explosives would be a lot more exiting.

Upriver small outboard motorboats floated and Jet Skis zipped and large-windowed houses towered at the shore, maximizing the water view. Overhead transmission lines carried power to the grid, that unfathomable tangle of consumers. And under the surface of the water, how many species struggled or thrived, having readjusted for better or worse in the past hundred years to slower warmer water? Take out a dam and what happens to all of this?

A week later, I read about Condit. Even in this season of the Elwha, even though I lived in the same state, I'd never heard of it before. The story was familiar. The Condit dam on the White Salmon River was old and inefficient—only 14 megawatts—and blocked the namesake fish completely from heading upriver. Oh, engineers had installed fish ladders at the start, way back in 1913, but they'd been poorly designed—it was, by all accounts, a tricky location in a deep gorge—and they'd washed out twice in floods. Since then, for a hundred years, there'd been no fish passage at all, and designing and installing a system now would cost way too much to pencil out. So after nearly thirty-five years of debate, the dam would be breached, right on the heels of the Elwha. The breaching itself interested me less than that thirty-five-year interlude.

A single photo accompanied the piece. A small prim woman in slacks and a long-sleeved blue blouse buttoned to the collar and at the cuffs, bespectacled and gray-permed, stood in a nook of a massive moss-covered cedar and grinned. The image was striking, mesmerizing, for the way the tree seemed to dwarf and delight her at once. The caption explained that eighty-seven-year-old Phyllis Clausen had been among those working to bring down Condit dam since 1976. If anyone could answer my questions, I thought, she could.

3

Revisit

Death Valley, California—November 2011

In the mobile trailer visitor center, the woman behind the desk wearing a polo shirt embossed with the Death Valley Natural History Association logo looked bored, nearly disdainful, and if I was not mistaken, distinctly Indian.

I approached the desk.

"Are there any books about the Timbisha Shoshone?"

"No."

"Where can I find out about the Homeland Act?"

"It's on the map."

Laurie and I had traveled to Death Valley along the same route my mother and I had taken in March. If that trip had been a tourist junket, this was a bona fide pilgrimage. Or something close. After months of communication missteps, I'd convinced myself that this would be the only way to get the homeland story unfiltered: to show up and ask around until somehow—who knew how?—I could talk to the Timbisha. Now I had my chance, and it was not going well.

"What do you want to know?" she asked.

"Did it make a difference?"

She made eye contact for the first time.

"We got our land. My mother and grandmother lived here. Now I live here."

Tourists approached and bought trinkets while I stood to the side sweating. I'd worn respectable clothes—a shirt with a collar, at least, and long pants rather than shorts—as though my clothes might indicate seriousness of purpose. If only to myself. Already, before 9:00 a.m., I regretted the decision. The temperature had to be pushing ninety. She made a transaction, sold a rust-orange baseball cap with a scorpion on it. Of all the colors that bleed into the landscape at that flat-light hour of the day, rust-orange was not one of them.

"How many Timbisha live here now?"

She shrugged.

"A hundred?"

"Less than that."

More silence. I had nothing to lose. I told her how I'd been trying to contact the tribe via letters, emails, phone calls. I'd found a website and had written to every person on the tribal council. But I'd been ignored. She listened and shook her head.

"They've taken over."

"Who?"

"The Bishop people."

The tribal council, she explained, had moved the whole operation 160 miles northwest to Bishop, taking everything with them.

"Everything?"

More visitors approached to buy postcards, and she waited for them to leave before she replied.

"Those people," she said with fury, "are almost white."

I thought she meant the tourists, but I realized in a moment that she meant the tribal leadership. She pulled out a small local phone book and looked up a number. She wrote with a pencil on a scrap of paper and handed it to me.

"That's who you should talk to," she said. "Barbara and Pauline."

If there were two people in Death Valley I wanted to talk to, they were Barbara Durham and Pauline Esteves. I'd known about Pauline Esteves for months, and I'd been hearing about Barbara Durham, too, a woman a generation younger than Esteves, who'd grown up in Furnace Creek, left to go to college, and returned as the land negotiations were beginning in earnest. Back home in Stehekin, I'd read a Park Service administrative history that shed some light on the long saga.

In the late 1980s, the California Desert Protection Act was on the verge of passing. The landmark legislation would double the size of Death Valley and designate it a national park rather than a national monument, which it had been since the 1930s. That meant protections would be stricter, and while the Timbisha Shoshone were glad enough for strict protections—they'd long opposed mining and nuclear waste disposal and other abuses—they also feared, rightly, the act would make it harder for them to reclaim land. So they went to work. Barbara Durham headed for a conference on Indian rights where she met Senator Daniel Inouye. The Timbisha Shoshone needed help, she told him. They needed an amendment to the California Desert Protection Act, and they needed one fast.

Inouye listened. When the act passed, the very next week, it included Amendment 705b, which ensured "access for traditional and religious purposes" and, more importantly, authorized a study to determine what lands might be "suitable for a reservation." The amendment didn't authorize land transfer per se. Didn't fund it either. But it did specify the study. To the Timbisha, this seemed like a victory. At first.

They waited for talks to be scheduled and waited some more. They even tried an end run. They started their own committee, scheduled their own talks, and wrote to Secretary of the Interior Bruce Babbitt to invite him to attend. Babbitt did not reply. So the tribe tried closer to home; they sent a letter to the brand-new superintendent of Death Valley National Park, Dick Martin.

To get this much straight I'd read the history three or four times. Not that it was poorly written or unclear, just that the saga grew more convoluted with every step. I thought I could use more personal insights, so I got in touch with an old Park Service friend who gave me a list of names and contact numbers.

"Be sure to talk to Dick Martin," he said.

I called Martin a month before my trip. A native North Dakotan, he came across Midwest polite with a heavy dose of western candor. He'd always considered himself a wilderness guy, he said, so he was delighted that the California Desert Protection Act had passed. But it didn't make his new job any easier. When he first arrived in Death Valley as superintendent, he had his hands full.

"If there were a hundred things to do," he said, "I might've been able to get to fifty."

He was vaguely aware of the local Indians, sure. A couple of Timbisha guys worked maintenance, but he didn't have any personal relationship with them. The issue just wasn't on his radar until the letter arrived officially requesting that the Park Service begin the process that had been guaranteed right there in the California Desert Protection Act. Amendment 705b. Martin had never heard of it.

With hindsight, he figures his superiors probably had. Maybe they knew the danger of a headline-worthy precedent—Park Service gives land away to Indians!—or maybe they thought they'd let Martin handle it, bungle it even, and the whole messy problem would disappear. Whatever they thought, Martin forged ahead. He invited the Timbisha and officials from the Bureau of Land Management (BLM), the Bureau of Indian Affairs, the Forest Service, and Inyo County, and they all sat down in the park offices to talk. Right away it became clear that the tribe wanted land, and Martin had no authority to turn over land or even to discuss turning over land. That would fall to someone much higher up, but no one higher up was offering to take over the process, so he thought he'd do what he could do.

"I was naïve," he said quietly over the phone. With a hint of apology.

Naïve would be an understatement. And naïve was not how everyone saw it. How could he *not* have known they wanted land? Wasn't that what Amendment 705b was all about?

"Maybe they were saying that from the start, but I didn't hear it."

The Timbisha submitted a list of lands they deemed suitable for a reservation, including 5,000 acres at Furnace Creek and 750,000 on BLM land on the west edge of the park. To the land managers these numbers were preposterous.

But the concept itself, to Martin, was beginning to seem less so. Martin was a career ranger. He loved the national parks, but the way the park had treated the Timbisha, well, he had to admit that some of the history was appalling.

"We'd promise X and X wouldn't happen, and over time we became the enemy. The Park Service was very disliked, and me personally . . ." He let the sentence dangle.

He was also getting to know the local Timbisha a little better, Pauline Esteves especially. One day a swamp cooler broke down during a meeting, and all the attendees went out to stare at the unit, to scratch their heads. Pauline and Dick Martin knew a trick. Together they told the rest of the negotiators to step aside while they wedged a paper clip into just the right place and the cooler whirred back into action. They were the locals. They had something in common.

"And there was another time. Pauline and I and some people went out to Saline Valley where there are those clothing-optional hot springs."

The entourage pulled up in vans, and the rest of the negotiators hopped out and headed for the water. The Timbisha chairwoman and the Park Service superintendent stood cross-armed, leaning side by side against the vehicles in the sun.

"I said, 'I'm from North Dakota. I don't do this,' and Pauline said, 'I ain't gonna go over there,' and our relationship began to get Band-Aids on it."

The bigger issue, Martin decided, was that the Timbisha had credibility: they'd spent their lives there and they weren't going anywhere. So he redoubled his efforts. Pretty soon, he was flying around the country, to Washington D.C. and to San Francisco, trying to persuade people in the Park Service that the Timbisha deserved some land. To no avail.

"We'd spent half our lives fighting for these parks. To give them up? Well, some people were just totally against it."

The two sides continued meeting in the visitor center auditorium at Furnace Creek until one day in March 1996—a day that would later be deemed "notorious"—the auditorium was unavailable, so the proceedings were moved to the un-air-conditioned fire cache. Snacks were set out on a table—juice, coffee, cookies—but no one touched them. The day was hot, and the room was crowded, and there were not enough seats, so some attendees were invited to sit on upturned buckets. Including Pauline Esteves.

The buckets were the final straw.

"This is not very appropriate," Pauline announced. "Did we make a mistake and come to the wrong place or what?"

Since receiving federal recognition in the 1980s, the Timbisha Shoshone were officially a sovereign nation. These were supposed to be government-to-government negotiations, not a two-bit consultation in a too-hot garage with juice boxes and buckets for seats.

"Right now we are leaving," she said. "The whole council is going to leave."

Barbara Durham answered on the first ring.

I said I was interested in the Homeland Act and that the bookseller had given me the number, and I asked if she might have time to talk.

"Yeah, well, I'm going to the doctor today over in Bishop."

"What about Pauline?" I asked. "Do you know if Pauline is around?"

"She's going to the doctor, too."

I stood sweating in the parking lot outside the mobile trailer ranger station.

"Well, this might sound crazy, but I was wondering, could I just come say hello? Shake your hand? I admire what you've done so much and . . ."

"We're leaving right now," she said. "Do you do email? You can email me."

She gave me her email address and hung up.

I'd come so far to meet these women, to hear the story. Not from an administrative history. Not from a former superintendent. From them. So I got in the car and drove the half mile to Indian Village.

I drove past an elevation sign—100 feet below SEA LEVEL—and down a spur road and parked in front of two stucco buildings, spare and attractive, stone colored and flat-roofed, and completely deserted. A large sign in orange and blue read "Timbisha Tribal Office Hours Mon–Friday 9:00–4:30." Ten o'clock on a Tuesday. No one to be found. A late-model Honda Ridgeline sat in the lot. An empty ashtray sat by the door. A dozen single-wide trailers and modest houses sat under palms and mesquite trees, a splash of green in the desert under power poles laid out in a straight line toward the horizon like a perspective drawing. I walked the perimeter of the buildings, sandals scuffing, listening to ravens cry in the distance, and something felt creepy, sinister even. Only then did I notice a twitch of movement, a camera following me, a lone Cyclops swiveling on its perch. Why? The doors were bolted shut. Who would try to get in anyway? Who could pose such a threat? I watched a car pass, leaving a rooster tail of dust.

When Pauline Esteves and Barbara Durham walked into the second round of negotiations, they must have been skeptical. The first round, culminating with the fire cache debacle, had been a spectacular failure, and in its wake, a furious uproar ensued. Greenpeace became involved, supporting the Timbisha cause, as did several U.S. senators. Marches were marched; letters were penned. Dick Martin was burned in effigy. Meanwhile, in the press, the Timbisha Shoshone were denigrated, accused of ignorance and collusion at once, while behind closed doors in Washington D.C. fears simmered that this precedent could undermine America's best idea.

But there were reasons to be hopeful.

To start with, both sides culled their teams to a core. The previous lawyer for the Timbisha had been a hothead—his correspondence blistering, his tone unretractable—so now there was a new one. The government had been naïve at best and condescending at worst, so while Dick Martin remained on the team, there was a new chief negotiator from the regional office, John Reynolds.

Maybe most importantly, both sides agreed to bring in Charles Wilkinson as mediator. Wilkinson was a professor at the University of Colorado,

Reclaimers

an expert in Indian law, and a prolific author. His book *Blood Struggle*, subtitled *The Rise of Indian Nations*, lays out a civil rights movement every bit as dramatic and successful as that of blacks in the 1960s. His book introduced me to writers like Vine Deloria Jr., whose 1969 classic *Custer Died for Your Sins: An Indian Manifesto* is scathing and smart, righteous and persuasive. Wilkinson's voice is steadier, as an outsider and an academic, and tinged with awe that tribes have endured five excruciating centuries only to find themselves more powerful now than they've been in 150 years.

I chased down both Reynolds and Wilkinson by telephone.

Reynolds told me that Wilkinson was responsible for turning the negotiations around.

"What did John Reynolds mean by that?" I asked Wilkinson.

He paused before answering.

"I believe in getting people talking about their dreams," he said.

The Timbisha invited the Park Service officials to their community hall for the first meeting to underscore their even footing this time around. Wilkinson walked in on the very first day and asked everyone to make a list of their core values. If it seemed more like an exercise at a self-help retreat than a crucial step in tooth-and-nail negotiations, no one complained. They went around the table reading their values aloud, and John Reynolds, according to Wilkinson, gave a speech—a good speech, a heartfelt speech—about what land means to the National Park Service. When it was Pauline Esteves's turn, she stood and addressed Reynolds directly.

"Are you going to respect our heritage?"

"Yes," said Reynolds. He held eye contact.

"Are you going to respect our sovereignty?'

"Yes," said John Reynolds. He did not look away.

More questions followed, a long forceful litany, and to each John Reynolds responded "yes."

"That's when everything changed," Wilkinson said. "Pauline Esteves is such a sophisticated woman. I mean, she's one of the most sophisticated human beings I've ever met. Nothing could make her blink. But that made her blink."

Wilkinson said he knew right then there was enough mutual respect to get something done.

I asked John Reynolds if he remembered that. No, no, Reynolds said, he remembered another turning point, a few weeks later.

They were discussing a piece of BLM land, not terribly valuable land, hard and rocky and waterless. Esteves sat slumped in her chair, hands entwined, eyes closed.

"If you were dumb you'd think she was asleep," Reynolds said.

A young member of the Timbisha contingent named Spike Jackson was growing impatient. He knew the land wasn't worth much, so he said as much: Why bother? Just forget it.

Suddenly, Esteves sat straight up and pounded the table with her fist.

"Never forget, Spike," she said. "Land is land."

In fact, no one ever had forgotten. Not for a second.

Land is power and symbol. Land is what underlies culture. You can talk about dreams and values, talk about common ground, but land is what had been taken and land was what had to be returned. Now, at last, it was out in the open. Now everyone was on the same page. Something had to give.

In the middle of the day, the horizon shimmered in waves, like heat off asphalt, and the mountains rose steep, and as far as you could see, alluvial fans—those cone-shaped deposits of sediment, stream-built and stark, that frame the valley—reached into the sand like work-worn knuckles curling down. I'd returned from the Timbisha offices, and Laurie and I weren't talking about what I'd seen, weren't talking about Barbara and Pauline, weren't talking about the ridiculous notion that had brought us here, several hundred miles out of our way, the notion that somehow I'd find these women just like that.

"We could stay another day," she said. "If there's a chance you could see them."

I went back inside to ask the bookseller about a place to stay. We hadn't brought camping gear, and the Furnace Creek Lodge was way out of our price range.

"Beatty," she said. "You can get a room there for cheap. It's only an hour."

She handed me a sheet listing motels and prices, and I called and left a message for Barbara, asking her to call.

I changed clothes in the passenger seat, and we set out walking across the flat sand, through gullies salt-crusted into honeycomb hexagons and tracked by illegal mountain bikers who apparently couldn't resist the allure of empty space. We left footprints in sand and gazed up at pinyons on the mountainsides and across at the mesquite in Timbisha Village, still visible from miles away.

Experiencing the desert like this—alone or mostly so, and far from home—reinforces the myth that it's inhospitable. An empty place. A moonscape. A wilderness. Even Dick Martin called it a wilderness. But a wilderness is the polar opposite of home. That dichotomy lay at the heart of the Homeland Act negotiations. If the National Park Service was to cede undeveloped land to people, however deserving, wasn't it also ceding an ideal, a core belief in the sanctity of unpeopled places? On the other hand, the Timbisha and those who supported them believed that "undeveloped" need not be synonymous with "uninhabited" and that ceding the land might nudge non–Native Americans toward a more nuanced understanding of the relationship between people and places, the kind of relationship that has been built over millennia, not decades, the kind that need not cause damage. The negotiations must have been agonizing, I thought, driven in part by the pervasive fear that losing communal grip on protected places could pave the way for exploitation.

After the initial meeting, the second-round negotiations moved to Las Vegas, perhaps the most unfitting setting imaginable. Here they were discussing the best use of land, in both an ecological and moral sense, in a place where, on display everywhere, you could find evidence of the worst: the gaudy neon, the high-ceilinged air-conditioned spaces, fountains spewing, all thanks to Hoover Dam and the Mafia.

Among the rules that Charles Wilkinson laid out at the beginning was that any time anyone on either side wanted to call for a break they could do so. And they did. Not infrequently. Not often. But as necessary.

They'd leave the air-conditioning and pace around the walkways that sur-rounded the hotel and let things settle.

One of those breaks made all the difference.

It was a day late in the negotiations, and the number of acres to be transferred was the only serious issue remaining. Reynolds had gotten the okay to relinquish land if the total was less than three hundred acres total. Problem was, the tribe had adopted that number, too, as the bare minimum: three hundred. There were other issues, plenty of them: the 7,500 acres of BLM land to be transferred, and the associated water rights, the 5,000 acres that would be designated as a Mesquite Use Area. But in the end, as in the beginning, the park land was what mattered, symbol-ically and actually. More than three hundred. Less then three hundred. Round and round it went.

Charles Wilkinson called for a break.

John Reynolds went walking the corridors. Vegas hotels are worlds in themselves, alive by night, hungover by day; tourists lounge beside pools in dark glasses reading thrillers, soaking up sun that heals and damages at once, others stay indoors in neon-lit casinos or drape-darkened rented rooms where the sun is made irrelevant by sheer force of will. Reynolds paced in the shade, under covered walkways. He wasn't hopeful, and he wasn't frustrated. He was weary—the negotiations were so very close—and he was lost in thought when he came around a corner and right there walking the opposite way came Pauline Esteves.

They faced each other and began to talk numbers. There was a twen-ty-five-acre buffer of land adjacent to the existing village that could not be developed due to a previously existing easement with the concessionaire, the company that ran the lodge and golf course. If he included that in the land transfer, would she agree? Because if she would, even though it would kick the final number up over the three-hundred-acre bar, he thought he could sell that.

She said yes.

So it was decided: 314 acres of National Park Service land, alongside 7,500 acres from the Bureau of Land Management, would go to the Tim-bisha Shoshone.

Reclaimers

It took most of a year for the bill to make it through both houses of Congress. With some prescience, Harry Reid of Nevada held it up with concerns about gaming on the new reservation, but that October the House passed the Timbisha Shoshone Homeland Act. President Bill Clinton signed it on November 1, 2000, and a celebration was held shortly thereafter in Furnace Creek. John Reynolds arrived bearing gifts of turtles carved from pipestone, Sioux symbols of the power of good, mementos of his first encounters with Native Americans as a child in Minnesota. Food was served, and speeches given. Then the dignitaries left and the Timbisha were on their own.

Everyone I'd talked to so far claimed the Homeland Act was an unmitigated success.

"The lesson," Dick Martin said, "is perseverance. When things get bleak, rope in as many good people as you can." He paused, this man who was once burned in effigy, and added softly, "I remember the experience fondly."

"It's gotta be the most satisfying thing I ever did," John Reynolds said. "Or right up there."

I wondered if Pauline Esteves or Barbara Durham would say the same thing.

Late afternoon and no returned call.

To stall a few hours more, we drove to Scotty's Castle. The former rich man's idyll, built in the 1930s in part by Timbisha laborers, remains a site of fascination for tourists—the half-apocryphal tale of Scotty himself, the lovable con man for whom the "castle" is named, is far better known and documented than Timbisha history—though the Park Service seems not to know what to do with it. Desert plants had been arranged not quite artfully in the former swimming pool. One lone maintenance employee raked gravel by a former bunkhouse. Inside, a ranger in period costume—a long-tailed suit coat and ruffled cuffs—awaited questions about the former grandeur while outside a horde of kids chased a coyote across a brown lawn.

We followed the long shoulderless road back toward Furnace Creek as the sun slipped lower in the west. This dramatic shifting light must be what brings artists here, I thought, and maybe what causes accidents, too. The main cause of death in Death Valley, according to park brochures, is the single-car accident. Do not depend on cell phones, they warn, or on GPS, which can show roads or trails where there are none. We stayed well within the white edge of the road, and stopped only once in a small grove of mesquites to look for the pods. The number of trees was few, the pods even fewer. If we had to survive on mesquite beans, we would starve.

I called Barbara Durham again, and let the land line ring long. I was ready to give up.

So we turned off, out of the park, toward Beatty to the east, the sky reflecting the sunset in swaths of orange and pink that grew redder and redder against the blue, and we rented a room at a hotel/casino, and we were glad enough to have a place to stay, though I regretted not having brought a tent. I collapsed on the bed, checked messages, then called again. No one picked up. I didn't leave another message.

For dinner our only choice was a downstairs Denny's in a windowless room off the casino. Our waitress was sun-weathered, bleach blond, and willow-thin, the epitome of a California desert rat. She asked about our day and told us how she worked down in Furnace Creek for eight years, raised her kids there alone, and now she was raising grandchildren and thought being closer to school here in town made sense, but she missed it, missed it something awful.

"Did you know any Timbisha?" I asked.

She didn't recognize the word.

"Shoshone?"

She knew some people with that last name.

"Were they Indians?" I asked.

She looked at me blankly.

"Indians," she said finally. "Yeah, I worked at the golf course, you know, and when we lost balls over the fence, we called them 'Indian bullets' because these old Indian ladies used to chuck them right back at us." She smiled a little. "You never saw them, but you knew they were there."

4

Remediation

Stehekin, Washington—November–December 2011

After the trip to Death Valley, home looked different. In part because, in many ways, Stehekin *is* different these days from the place where Laurie and I landed, by youthful happenstance, twenty-five years ago. Startlingly so. The changes aren't the ones you see in the cities: more development, freeways, storefronts come and gone, skyscrapers raised and razed. Though some old-timers still bristle at mention of the arrival of electricity in the 1960s or the paved road in the 1970s or the satellite dishes in the early 2000s, the most obvious changes lie on the land itself. Along Lake Chelan, tens of thousands of acres have burned in the past two decades. Fire scientists take a long view, admiring the so-called mosaic—some sections burned to black, some singed and recovered, some relatively untouched—but there's no denying that, on balance, the greenness, the overwhelming lushness that we humans take comfort in for whatever reason, has given way to miles of snags, gray as whiskers. The threat of fire has become the reality of fire. Ditto for floods. The river, which defines the valley, has shifted in some places by hundreds of yards, overtaken homes and washed out roads. New logjams outpace new homes, in size and number, tenfold. Telltale cones of stringy once-wet debris around tree bases remind us of the water level, once and future.

The unspoken culprit is, of course, climate change. Here as elsewhere. You can split hairs over how to take care of nature or take back nature, over who might do it best or how or why, but maybe the point is moot. I have friends who've staked their lives on convincing people of the threat of human-caused climate change. Sometimes I chided myself that the question I kept asking—How can we live right on earth?—paled in comparison with theirs: How can we stop destroying the earth? Certainly not by driving thousands of miles in a Buick. But that's exactly what I'd been doing. I'd been doing it out of a kind of desperation that doesn't always abide logic, and around every corner, there'd been a surprise.

Like Mono Lake. On the way north, no one had been on the road, not in Nevada and not in California either, where a construction detour sent us westward along a plateau of bentonite clay that rose and dropped like a roller coaster until there it was, blue and wide and expansive: Mono Lake.

I was shocked.

Back when I'd drive to college from Southern California to Oregon, the lake starred in my own personal state-of-the-planet newsreel, the symbol of all that had gone wrong in my home state. In the late 1980s, the wide shallow lake at the base of the Sierras was almost completely dry: a white-edged cobalt puddle in the middle of a dust bowl. If I didn't know exactly what had happened, it wasn't hard to guess. I'd just left greater Los Angeles, a sprawling half-state chock-full of people in need of water, not just for the easy-to-scorn swimming pools and golf courses and air-conditioned malls, but for schools and hospitals and churches and homes. Not to mention farms. Every single human activity required water, so what could be done? Nothing, I thought. Nothing at all. Driving past the empty lake fueled my sense of futility. Like the omnipresent smog of my childhood, the situation at Mono Lake seemed like one more symptom of a degenerative disease with only one way to go: down.

Now, twenty-five years later, the lake stretched blue and wide and full, or nearly so. Laurie was as shocked as I was—she'd spent time in the Sierras in the early 1980s taking a course in environmental history in which the sad fate of the lake loomed large—so even though we were in a hurry to reach a friend's house, we pulled off and headed for the shore where a small crowd of tourists congregated. Many were taking pictures of the tufas, the calcium-bearing springs that well up through the alkaline water, unlikely Dr. Seuss extrusions, some as old as 13,000 years, through which ducks floated.

As we hiked through rabbitbrush and toward the water, I wondered: Who made this happen? A flyer on the bulletin board told the story.

In 1974, a graduate student and avid birder named David Gaines began to study the lake, and he returned with an entire cadre two years later. Their findings showed that since the City of Los Angeles had begun siphoning water from the lake in 1941, the lake had dropped forty-two feet and the tributaries that fed it had run dry. As a result a whole interconnected web of species dependent on the alkaline balance of baking soda, Epsom salts, and lye was threatened. What's more, the lake had been a critical stopping point for hundreds of species of migrating birds, some that nested, others that feasted on the brine shrimp. They, too, suffered from the lake loss.

The study might've been enough to fuel change, but Gaines was not about to count on that. He and his future wife, Sally Judy, and a friend, David Winkler, formed the Mono Lake Committee, and the young activists embarked on a driving tour showing slides and passing out bumper stickers that read "Save Mono Lake."

"Do you remember those?" Laurie asked.

I did. They were ubiquitous in the late 1970s—I'd see them on VW vans and sometimes Mercedeses in Southern California—and the fact that so little had changed by the time of my college commutes fueled my despair. Turns out, my problem was impatience. I wasn't thinking long-term. The youthful reclaimers were.

The Mono Lake Committee convinced the Audubon Society to sue the City of Los Angeles—three grad students suing the second-biggest city in the nation—in the first in a series of lawsuits that alleged the water diversions violated the public trust. Four years later, the California Supreme Court ruled in favor of the plaintiffs. That is, they ruled that the state had an obligation to protect such places as Mono Lake "as far as feasible." What that meant, exactly, provoked debate and negotiation and foot-dragging.

The arduous process lasted fifteen years. Not until 1994—five years after David Gaines died in a car wreck—did the state issue an order to raise the lake level. David Gaines may not have lived to see the success, but they'd done it, he and his friends.

The numbers are deceiving. As Laurie and I followed a trail of signs marking where exactly these levels lay, we saw how, in a shallow lake, a vertical foot or two in elevation means a whole lot of square acreage of water.

In 1941, when diversions began, the surface of Mono Lake was 6,417 feet above sea level.

By 1982, at its low point, it was down to 6,372 feet above sea level.

In 2011, it was 6,383 feet above sea level. On its way up again.

The numbers, in other words, understate the drama, which played out as we walked several hundred feet between level markers, and the effect, which plays out in the number of migratory birds that continue to return, more than eighty species including phalaropes and grebes and snowy plovers, plus the two nesting species of California gulls. The Mono Lake Committee, now 16,000 members strong, sponsors Restoration Wednesdays, when volunteers pull invasive plants and water Jeffrey pine seedlings along the intake creeks.

The story read like another unmitigated triumph. Except that, like nearly everything in nature these days, it is mitigated. The highest proposed "future management level" for the lake—the mandated level—will be 6,392 feet above sea level. The lake will forever remain twenty-five feet below its historic level.

Considering how dire the situation had been, that seemed a reasonable goal, even an impressive accomplishment—certainly more than I'd ever imagined possible—but I found when we got home that the Mono Lake Committee offers this sobering advice on its website: "Perhaps the greatest lesson of Mono Lake is that it is always better to prevent damage than to rely on restoration."

The quote stayed with me as fall rains descended in Stehekin, and snow accumulated on the peaks then melted, and the river rose, growing into familiar latte froth, and still the most immediate problem was neither the weather nor the climate, but politics. The Stehekin River Management Plan inched toward approval, and the National Park Service—my former employer, Laurie's current one—was asking for public feedback.

Neighbors busily composed letters of response. Most focused on land acquisition. A rating system in the plan showed which private properties were of the highest value to the federal government. There was practical benefit to this: If your land were to get heavily flooded, say, it would be to the benefit of the Park Service to acquire it and get the human detritus out of the way of the river, while it would be to your benefit to have a willing buyer if it got to the point where no private party would be dumb enough to purchase it. But to many people the word "acquisition" had a sinister ring. The threat of a government takeover, in their eyes, loomed large.

For Laurie and me, the problem was more urgent. When we built our house on high ground, we'd banked, literally, on our high bank. We hoped the huge boulders we'd encountered digging the foundation would secure us twenty feet above the road no matter how close floods came, or how big. But what if the bank proved less sturdy? What if only river rubble lay under the surface? We'd seen as much elsewhere in the valley where banks much higher than ours were washed away in a flash. If it came to that, if the river came charging at our bank, then we'd always believed we held one ace in the hole: the road.

Here's how it would work: The National Park Service cannot, by mandate, protect private property from flooding, but it can protect a public road. The Stehekin Valley Road lay, like an international boundary or a damned good insurance policy, between us and the river. The fact that it did had been a big reason why we'd chosen to buy this particular piece of property. Now the Stehekin River Management Plan called for the road to be moved behind our house. That would almost certainly prevent damage to the road, but it would potentially allow damage to our house.

So, we should have opposed the proposal, but we couldn't. It didn't make sense. With climate change, the river would keep flooding, the road would keep washing out, and eventually money for reconstruction would dry up. Or political will would. To make matters worse, our property, for now, lay in the middle range of the rating system, not yet threatened enough to be high, and who knew if that would change with so much opposition to acquisition? The situation was complicated and getting more so with every season. We knew what was at stake, but we wanted to do what was right, and trying to balance the two was excruciating.

I started a response letter, but could not finish.

Instead we headed to Holden Village for homecoming. Holden, nestled in a narrow valley two thousand feet above Lake Chelan, is the closest community to Stehekin and a world away. In the 1940s Holden was an active mine. Not just any mine, but a massive one, providing most of the copper for bullets during World War II. At its peak, the mine processed two thousand tons of copper a day. It was an iconic western experience, one that's still romanticized plenty—individualistic, dangerous, and lucrative—in part because it was so short-lived. The mine went belly-up in 1957, when the price of copper dropped precipitously, and when it did, some people claim, the miners left everything exactly as it was—an unfinished card game on a table and work boots by the door—and got the hell out.

A few years later, the Lutheran church took over. Holden Village, an affiliate of the church, now uses the mine's dormitories to house summer guests who come from all over the country, especially the upper Midwest, for programs on spirituality, politics, science, and arts, not to mention for hiking in mountains as dramatic as any on the continent. The ethic is progressive and communal. Visitors strip their own beds and clear their own plates, attend nightly vespers, and love the place with a passion. On the Lake Chelan ferry, it's easy to pick the Holdenites out. They are Scandinavian blond and Midwest courteous. When the ferry docks at Lucerne, where people headed to Holden disembark, passengers line up to pass luggage hand to hand up the ramp in a human chain. (By contrast, when you land at Stehekin, people scatter like cattle from a pen.) And if you take the rickety school bus twelve miles up the curvy road from the lake following the steep gorge of Railroad Creek—fed by multiple glaciers, it's the kind of "creek" that would be called a "river" any place but here—

to Holden Village itself, the manicured lawns and ice cream shop and bowling alley make the place seem more like a small liberal arts college campus than an old mining town.

There's more. When you arrive at Holden, everyone in town lines up and waves in greeting like the chorus in a musical.

That's exactly what they did when Laurie and I arrived with twenty or so of our Stehekin neighbors. They lined the road and waved their arms in welcome, a motley hippie-church crowd: men in Carhartts, women in flowing skirts, plenty of fleece. Homecoming is an annual event designed to foster fellowship: two nights packed with preplanned fun. There used to be a rubber chicken football game, and once there'd been an art show that showcased the work of Holden's many aspiring painters and photographers and weavers and musicians. Some years you could ski—a boon, since snow in early winter is rarely skiable at home—and always the kids could play ping pong and fill up on free cinnamon toast in the dining hall. The event is makeshift and laid-back and family-oriented. But this time it would be different.

The village buzzed with industrial activity. Just beyond the eager greeters, workers in hard hats and steel-toe boots—an imported labor force, distinctly un-Holden-like and from what I could tell, entirely male—huddled in small groups, arms folded. D-6 cats prowled the roads, grading boneyards and turnarounds. An excavator worked at demolishing a steel skeleton three stories high. Turns out, not surprisingly, that when the miners ditched town, card games and boots weren't all they left behind: there were the poisonous heavy metal tailings—copper, cadmium, zinc, aluminum, and iron—enough to get Holden listed as a Superfund site. There'd been talk of a cleanup for so many years that we'd stopped believing it would ever happen. Now it was happening. Remediation, they called it.

"What do you think that means?" I asked no one in particular as our small group of Stehekinites hauled luggage into the dorms.

No one replied. There was unease among us, as though forces out of our control surrounded us—we had plenty of those back home—and they were not worth discussing.

In place of rubber chicken football, we played an elaborate version of capture the flag that featured soccer balls, chunks of firewood, costumes. We played until near dark in finger-aching cold to the sound of kids laughing and Railroad Creek rushing and the omnipresent beeping back-up alarms of diesel machinery. The workers were working, not playing games. The Holdenites called them miners, and it made a kind of sense. The contract employees were paid higher wages in a week, in most cases, than Holden volunteers make in a summer. Some had left the oil fields of North Dakota, others had been mining in Peru.

In the morning, the miners' breakfast consisted of bacon, sausage, eggs, fried potatoes with cheese, and pancakes; the Lutherans' breakfast, served an hour later, consisted of oatmeal, toast, and peanut butter. The kids discovered the difference when they rose early: an enormous spread of calories available for the taking. Soon, we'd all heard. The miners weren't really miners, just regular people in search of a paycheck, and the Lutherans were not necessarily Lutherans either, just regular people in search of something more. Twenty of us from Stehekin might be guests of the Lutherans, but we were opportunists. Once word was out, we ate with the miners. Then we had to walk it off.

With a couple of friends, Laurie and I left the families to the ping pong table and the arts and crafts projects and hiked alongside a chain-link fence to switchbacks covered in an icy skiff of snow, speckled with the yellow needles of larches, curled and wispy. The day was cold, too cold to shed our down coats even while hiking uphill, and as we approached the trail's end in a high alpine basin surrounded by granite cliffs and avalanche chutes and peaks unseen behind ridges behind ridges, Laurie— the realist among us, and the coldest one, too—gathered sticks for a small warming fire. We started the fire atop talus and sipped from near-frozen water bottles and told stories and laughed. At that moment it was easy to imagine why, when midwesterners come to Holden, they might believe they've escaped, that they are in a better, safer, more pristine world. When in fact it's the precise opposite.

The numbers for the remediation are staggering. The mining operation left ten million tons of tailings spread over ninety acres, and fifty-two miles of tunnels discharging heavy metals directly into Railroad Creek. The mining company, Rio Tinto, a subsidiary of a multinational based in the United Kingdom, will pay costs of $107 million over five years, with oversight and direction from the Forest Service, Washington State, the Yakama Nation, and the Environmental Protection Agency.

"The worthless waste," reads literature from the heyday of the mine, "is washed away at the bottom of the cell."

But there was no away. There is no away. Pollutants go into the creek and end up in Lake Chelan. That's what makes the clean-up process remediation, I'd learn. It's the language of Superfund, the shorthand name for the Comprehensive Environmental Response, Compensation, and Liability Act of 1980, which requires the removal of contaminants that pose grave danger to the environment and to human health. Period. No one pretends Superfund projects aspire to restore anything Mono Lake–style. They just want to remove the pollutants. Strike that: they *have* to remove the pollutants; it's the law.

But it's never easy. They can't actually remove anything at Holden Village. Engineers determined they could not risk disturbing the tailings on land since toxins would then be airborne and volatile. Instead, they'll cover the contaminated acres—"cap" them—with topsoil and plant trees atop. The waterborne tailings pose a more difficult problem. The plan requires the mining company to shift the entire Railroad Creek watershed away from the tunnels and install a water purification plant. It's hard to know whether the remediation will work or whether it's necessary; many local people are skeptical. Others take the more practical stance: hell, it's jobs; over a thousand people showed up at a job fair midwinter. Remediation is not reclamation. It has no higher goal: not putting right, not making useful. It's just a remedy, a fix, an uber-expensive apology, and it may very well be crucial prevention of more damage. Still, when you're standing in the shadow of granite grandeur watching from above as a D-6 carves a turnaround, it's depressing.

The next morning we re-walked the gauntlet of well-wishers to board an old school bus, this one with the name "Honey" hand-painted on the side and tires missing rubber cogs and wool blankets draped over each bench seat, for the chilly ride down. Stehekin kids returned to knitting hats with yarn they dyed themselves, and I returned to fretting about the river plan, trying to figure out how best to balance damage and change, responsibility and safety, ecological sensitivity and plain good sense. After forty minutes, we reached the spit of land at the base of the road where we'd wait for the ferry to take us home.

Railroad Creek ran green and clear, the edges hoar-frosted. Near the outlet, the kids congregated to play beside a barely frozen pool. They pried up thin sheets of ice from the edge, the size and shape of house windows, glove-handled them, and karate-kicked them into shards, over and over, then skidded toward the water to toss the shards Frisbee-style into the lake, farther and then farther yet, daring each other, testing the limits. At last, one mother sighed and headed out to break up the fun. A kid with icy, soaked clothes, after all, would be a serious problem. Other mothers tried to restrain and console her. They knew the truth: as nice as the idea of prevention might sound, once a frenzy begins, it's nearly impossible to make it stop.

5

Talk Talk

Whidbey Island, Washington—January 2012

The Mountain Maidu ("my-doo") live in the Northern Sierras in a corner of California so remote many Californians don't know it exists; it's drier than the redwood country to the west and more lush, much more, than the spare expanse of basin and range in Nevada to the east. The Maidu, who divide themselves into valley, foothill, and mountain tribes, once were a rich tribe with salmon and trout in the rivers and plenty of wild game—deer, bear, elk, and wild turkey—and acorns, the mainstay of their diet, in the forest. They made exquisite baskets from gray willow and cottonwood and bear grass. The Mountain Maidu lived in small settlements in High Sierra valleys along tributaries of the Feather River; they weathered hard winters and thrived in summer. But like Native Americans everywhere, they experienced unimaginable losses over two centuries: their land stolen, their rivers dammed, their people killed or dispersed. Current membership stands at about 2,000, which is either shockingly low compared to the 310,000 Indians estimated to have lived in California before the gold rush or shockingly high considering what they've endured. Most of the Mountain Maidu lack federal recognition—the hard-won status that gives tribes sovereignty, allowing them to make and enforce laws and, usually, to reclaim land—and many live poorly, but they're still here.

And so, it turns out, is their traditional knowledge. At least some of it. In 1998, Congress sent out a nationwide call for programs to test "alternative techniques" on national forests, so the Maidu submitted a proposal using a brand-new acronym getting bandied about in land management circles: TEK. Traditional ecological knowledge. The Forest Service snapped it right up.

The story intrigued me: not just taking back land, but trying to make it better, despite ownership, despite everything, through work. That, more than anything, drew me in. The restoration at Mono Lake, the remediation at Holden, even the land reclamation in Death Valley—the aftermath at least—seemed dictated, for better and worse, by complex politics. If politics sometimes baffled me, work I could relate to, especially work in the woods—all those years clearing trails with chainsaws and axes and pruners—and the little I'd learned about TEK was all about work. The basic tenet was that humans have always worked the land, used it, and therefore the methods for using it best—"sustainably" is the buzzword—lies with those who've worked it longest in specific places with specific knowledge. I arranged to speak to Lorena Gorbet, the sixty-five-year-old director of the Maidu Cultural and Development Group, on the telephone. But since we don't have telephones in Stehekin, we had to wait until I went to work—teaching in this case—on the other side of the Cascades.

A few weeks later, I sat in a motel room on Whidbey Island with a view across Puget Sound to Mount Baker talking to her in Arizona, where she lives in winter now that she's retired and her arthritis worsens in the cold. Neither of us, ironically enough, was in the place we know and love best. I was hoping we could talk about work. Instead she wanted to talk about talk.

When she first met with land managers, she said, to discuss setting up a Mountain Maidu–run stewardship program on the Plumas and Lassen National Forests, the government officials started talking deadlines and quotas, treatments and acres, the kinds of details that must go into a contract. What, exactly, did the Mountain Maidu plan to do? They didn't know yet, she told them. They'd have to go visit their relations and see what they had to say. By relations, Gorbet did not mean the tribal elders or even the board of the nonprofit she directs. She meant: the plants, the animals, the air, the wind, the water.

"We needed to talk to them," she said, "and listen and find out what they needed."

This was, by Forest Service standards, crazy talk.

"See, we take care of the trees and animals and rocks and birds same as family members and in turn they take care of us," Gorbet explained. "All we wanted was to talk to our relations."

"What did they say?" I asked.

"The place was hurting. In Forest Service terms it had been heavily impacted."

She used the phrase "heavily impacted" as though the translation might help me understand. And it did. The 2,100 acres for which the Maidu would take responsibility had been impacted, she explained, by illegal dumping, off-highway vehicle use, fire suppression, then huge devastating fires, too much logging, then too little. A highway ran through it, a railroad, too. In the woods the trees had grown tight and dark and silent. No birds singing, no animals rustling.

"Not like Humbug Valley," she said. "Humbug Valley is pristine."

I'd never heard of Humbug Valley and had no idea why she was bringing it up. I scribbled the name in my notebook, underlined it three times and returned to the story at hand. "What did your relations want you to do?"

"Let the sunlight in, let those tender plants grow, open it up to breathe." The Forest Service, Gorbet pointed out, was interested only in conifers. Foresters made a regular practice of clearing underbrush while the Maidu wanted to cultivate the berries for food and the willow and maple, too, for basketry. They wanted to prune oaks to encourage bushi-ness and low branches to increase the harvest of acorns. Perhaps most of all, they wanted to reintroduce fire to let sunlight in, to allow tender green plants to grow, to give the trees a little breathing room. Here the Forest Service and the Maidu were in complete agreement. Only difference was, the Maidu had history on their side.

Diggers. That's what California Indians used to be called. Textbooks describe them as small, loosely organized bands that spoke over a hundred languages but never made the big supposed evolutionary leap from hunting and gathering (and digging up roots, hence the name) to farming. These days scholars speculate that maybe frequent droughts kept them from planting staples like corn, beans, or squash, or maybe they preferred the more balanced diet that hunting and gathering provided, or maybe they chose a more seasonally balanced workload than all-summer farming would require. Whatever the reason, for decades, the Maidu and others were dismissed as Diggers.

Turns out, the problem wasn't just the ugly name; it was the whole concept, which was wrong wrong wrong. California Indians *did* cultivate wild plants, by harvesting, pruning, and coppicing (cutting trees down repeatedly to stumps to encourage regrowth of multiple shoots), and mostly by using fire. They'd burn in different seasons at different intensities for different effects. Pyrodiversity, it's called. Maybe, one theory holds, the so-called Diggers didn't become crop farmers because fire and farming didn't mix. And fire did a better job. With fire, California Indians could tend the entire landscape rather than particular crops.

"That's how we used to do it," Lorena Gorbet said over the phone. "The journals of Fremont and Kit Carson describe a forest that was open and park-like where you could walk three abreast, and that was not just natural, we kept it that way. We're finally getting people to see that."

So everyone agreed: Fire needed to be restored for forest health. But how much? And when? The fuel loading had grown too heavy to allow for the kind of broadcast burns the Maidu would have set off in the past. Instead they'd have to burn piles or set smaller, lower-intensity fires. But before they did, before a single match could be struck, they'd have to attend training, fill out paperwork, work through the compliance, file reports and reports and reports. Thinning required even more red tape. The profits from selectively harvested trees would need to be moved into stewardship trust. The whole process would require more personnel than the Forest Service had. And when the Maidu requested a ninety-nine-year contract? More crazy talk. Anyone who's ever dealt with a federal budget knows how it fluctuates. Nothing is certain year to year. Ninety-nine years? No way.

But even as the bureaucratic wheels creaked into motion, the Maidu went to work: thinning and burning where possible, yes, but also pruning willows for basketry and tending oaks to maximize acorn production. (The first time Forest Service officials came out and saw Maidu workers raking around the trees, they were baffled. "They said, 'You're not going to make any money doing that,'" Gorbet said with a laugh.) They held picnics and chili cook-offs and work parties where kids planted camas bulbs harvested, with permission, from nearby ranches.

"We could see the difference in bringing humans back right away. The other animals came back, too: bear, deer, mountain lion, beaver, wild turkeys," she said. "Even wild turkeys," she repeated.

When Lorena Gorbet talked about the turkeys, and every time she talked about her relations with such easy clarity, a lump lodged hard in my throat. Part of it was plain discomfort. I bristled at New Age stereotypes and the kinds of ideas behind *The Secret Life of Plants*, the best-selling 1970s manifesto that got housewives talking to houseplants. But there was more, too. All the talk about talk might be crazy in a way. But it's not that crazy. Anyone who's worked on the land—tucking seeds into soil, pruning roses back by leaves of five, harvesting morels or maples, tending apple trees or straight tall firs—knows this much: it takes time and patience to understand what works best, and while some broad concepts can be applied, the devil, so to speak, is in the details, and one of the details is how to talk about it.

Oh, we have plenty of words. Ecology for nature, community for people. Symbiosis for science, balance for the Buddhists. Big words, with big meanings that slip into and over one another, dimming and limning, like morning light shifting over the green fringe of forest where the trees have grown too tight, trying to find a way in.

"It's just part of your DNA, and you have to take care of it. Most Indian people feel this way," Lorena Gorbet said to me.

She said this in the patient, practiced way of someone who's been interviewed many times, but I knew what she meant. Indians have a different understanding of the natural world and a million ways to talk about it, as many ways as we have to talk about money or Jesus or baseball or literature. The things that we love. When Lorena Gorbet talked about her relations, she meant it in the same dead-serious way Catholics do when they say the Eucharist is the body of Christ. Not a figure of speech, not a metaphor. The real thing. The most real thing.

Lorena Gorbet told me that as a child she learned how her people had been herded off to boarding schools, how their culture had to hide underground. Her grandmother taught her the old ways, and she always warned her: don't tell anyone and don't show anyone. But times have changed. Now Gorbet talks all the time to anyone who will listen, especially kids. She tells them to go get reacquainted with their relations: the wind, the water, the fish, the birds, and the sky. She tells them: if we take care of them, they take care of us. Sometimes, she says, those kids go home and teach their parents.

She also keeps talking with the Forest Service, she said, though it's not always easy. The Maidu and the Forest Service spent more than a year setting up so-called communication protocols, a way to talk to one another. Then NEPA—the labyrinthine process required by the National Environmental Protection Act before any project on public land can proceed—took another three and a half years. Eventually, the two sides agreed on a ten-year contract.

I sat gazing at Mount Baker. Such a wrong name. The Lummi call it "Koma Kulshan," meaning "white mountain," which makes a lot more sense. I'd wanted the Maidu story to be all about work, but maybe, I thought, reclaiming the talk is more important.

I was wrong.

"That's why we need Humbug Valley," she said.

This time I didn't let the reference slip past me.

"Tell me about Humbug Valley."

Humbug, she explained, is one of those high valleys of the Sierras, at nearly 4,500 feet, and it's considered sacred by the Maidu.

"And it's still pristine."

She repeated this word—"pristine"—with wonder, near incredulity.

Starting in the 1920s, many of the tributaries of the Feather were flooded for hydropower and irrigation, but in Humbug Valley there wasn't enough water to justify a dam. So it was spared. Even now, Lorena told me, there is still a healthy forest in Humbug Valley, and a naturally carbonated spring that bubbles up at the base of a hillside surrounded by moss-covered boulders. There are grinding pits and graves, testament to the Maidu who've cherished it for so long.

Only problem is Humbug Valley has been owned, for the last hundred years, by Pacific Gas & Electric: PG&E.

"Plunder, grab, and extort," Gorbet quipped.

The Maidu hoped that was about to change. The huge utility went belly-up in 2001 as a result of the energy deregulation debacle and was directed, as a result, to sell off about a thousand parcels of land, including many in the Feather River basin. According to the bankruptcy settlement, about half of the land would go to the Federal Energy Regulatory Commission, but the rest would go to agencies or nonprofits to be managed for the public benefit. That included nearly eight thousand acres around Lake Almanor.

It also, miraculously, included Humbug Valley.

The Maidu wanted that land. Check that. They wanted that land *back*. Ownership would make everything so much easier. No need to write contracts or fill quotas. No need to ask permission to gather grass seed or hold a picnic.

"But first we had to get them to take us seriously."

Much of that work had to be done through the Maidu Summit Consortium. Nine established groups associated with the tribe had joined forces to form the nonprofit a few years earlier to try to circumvent the disadvantages of having no central governing body or common land base. Before they did, outsiders—government officials or private grant foundations—claimed they didn't know whom to talk to. There were so many different bands of Maidu, different factions. Not all of them were easy to get along with. Not all got along with one another.

"We got so tired of going to meetings where an official would ask 'Does everyone in the Maidu tribes agree?' Now, if we come with a resolution, they know we do."

Still, when it came to Humbug Valley, they had an uphill battle.

The first meeting the officials from Pacific Gas & Electric held was not exactly secret, but it wasn't open either. They'd assembled a group of interested parties to discuss the looming fate of lands around the Lake Almanor basin that the power company would relinquish. They'd invited a dozen or more officials from government agencies like the U.S. Forest Service and California Department of Fish and Game, and NGOs including Ducks Unlimited and CalTrout. The fact that they had not invited the Mountain Maidu was worse than an oversight; it was an affront. The fact that they'd chosen to meet in Humbug Valley was something worse than that. Not that it mattered. The Maidu were used to being excluded, and they knew exactly what to do.

Lorena Gorbet and her friend Beverly Ogle and a young man named Farrell Cunningham, only twenty-seven but an up-and-coming tribal leader and one of the last three remaining speakers of the Maidu language, showed up anyway.

"That," Lorena Gorbet said, "was only the beginning."

For years, the Maidu attended meetings and submitted proposals and completed projects in Humbug Valley aimed at proving themselves as capable and deserving of caring for the land as more-established entities. By the time we talked on the phone, the only other agency still in contention was the California Department of Fish and Game. If that agency were to take title, it'd be the 111th parcel in its control with part of a budget of hundreds of millions of dollars supported by the thirty-seven million residents of the great state of California. If the Maidu Summit were to get it, it'd be the first chunk of their homeland that the two thousand remaining Maidu have reclaimed. Ever.

I mentioned the Timbisha Shoshone in Death Valley, how they're an even smaller tribe, and they fought for federal recognition, and once they got it, they were able to get their land.

Gorbet shrugged it off.

"The problem with recognition," she said, "is that once you're a governmental entity you have a whole new set of problems." Problems like constitutions and councils and—eventually, inevitably—casinos. The

Maidu have fewer rights than the Timbisha, she said, but also fewer headaches. None of this, I began to realize, was straightforward.

Meanwhile, the stewardship program, in its eighth year, neared completion. The monitoring had yet to be completed. Not all the quotas had been met. The pragmatist in me still had nagging questions. In the end, how exactly did the work go? Was it any different from what a regular Forest Service crew might do?

But to Lorena Gorbet's way of thinking, the program had already been a success.

"The forest was dark and silent," she said. "Now it's alive with talk."

II

Face-to-Face

6

The Red Fox and the Tule Elk

Point Reyes, California—March 2012

A guest book at the writers' retreat claimed the gardens harbored a red fox, but the chances he'd show himself seemed slim since winter weather in Northern California had not yet loosed its hold in March. I'd planned this as a research trip: I thought I'd visit the Timbisha Shoshone in Death Valley and the Mountain Maidu in the Sierras, and then settle in for two weeks to make sense of what I'd learned. Only problem was, the dates I was offered at the retreat came before, not after, my road trip. I'd arrive with no new story to tell.

To make matters worse, the Buick broke down on my way south from Stehekin. Les Schwab fixed my brakes and three hundred bucks later I was back on the interstate, headed south past Mount Shasta and fence-mounted signs with hand-painted Tea Party slogans—American Revolution Now—and west into Marin, the richest and most liberal county in California, where a curvy pot-holed road wound for miles past dairy cows on green hills that undulated toward the edge of the Pacific, where I coasted to a stop, radiator steaming.

I walked on rubbery legs to stand with a crowd of windbreaker-clad tourists leaning against a chain link fence at an overlook, eyes fixed on the ocean with the mindless focus of ten-year-olds playing computer games. At intervals, they exclaimed like spectators at a fireworks show.

"What?" I asked. "Where?"

At first I saw nothing but blue.

The man standing beside me pointed a quarter mile offshore. At first I thought he did not speak English, but soon I realized he probably did, but that no one dared break the spell of communal silence. I squinted until I saw one hump rise, then another, then another. I saw twenty-five gray whales that day, more of this once-endangered species than I'd seen in my life.

From the parking lot the coastline splayed both directions in an unending Y. Waves like ruffles crashed onto sand or against cliffs beneath the green rolling hills like a scene from Ireland or Scotland. Point Reyes National Seashore was preserved, in part, because it belonged to the Coast Guard—the military as de facto protector for decades—and in part because of the persistence of conservation activists. The fact that they succeeded seemed, from that perspective, flabbergasting. It's one thing for conservationists to have snagged the rugged North Cascades back home. There's some valuable timber there, but getting it out would have been tough at best. Here you had oceanfront property in a state of thirty-seven million. I tried to guess the value of this real estate the way guys I used to work with tried to guess board footage of the old-growth fir we sawed out of the trail. Priceless would be an understatement.

I stopped on my way back inland to see baby elephant seals, another species nearly extinct a hundred years ago, lounging in a protected cove. One stared long at me, big-eyed, then laid a single fin companionably, or maybe protectively, over another pup asleep next to him. There's an argument that preservation cages up land, keeping it from people who need affordable places to live. I grew up with the kind of class consciousness that sees those curvy one-lane roads in Marin as a way to, more or less, keep the riffraff out. Who can commute to work on roads like that? (For the entire next two weeks in Marin, in fact, I couldn't shake the discomfort. I felt grateful and privileged and decidedly out of place.) That prejudice, I knew, lay somewhere at the root of my insistent focus on usefulness. Do you mean useful only for humans? my friends would sometimes ask. I held firm. Yes, yes, that's what it's about. We can be as altruistic as we'd like toward other species—we must be—but we can't pretend to ignore the needs of our own. But standing there in front of the seal pup, holding eye contact for so long, the oversimplification—do baby elephant seals really need this place more than human children do?—suddenly seemed hollow and silly and utterly lacking in compassion. The pup lifted a fin to scratch its chin, and then flipped to its other side.

Two other writers shared a house with me overlooking Tomales Bay. We ate supper together in the evening; the rest of the time we worked alone beside electric space heaters in private huts. The sun shone the day we arrived, and the next day conceded to thick gray gauze that stuck as long as we stayed. Rain fell in torrents and leaked through the roof. From inside my hut, I gazed out at tidal flats. Even the shorebirds, huddled shoulder to shoulder, seemed afflicted as they stood on mud flats below the house awaiting the tide. When the water rose, the whole lot of them—sandpipers, godwits, plovers, goldeneyes and coots, the occasional egret or heron—skittered in concentric circles like swifts in the air as I watched through binoculars.

I tried to write, but mostly I read. I read books about dams and articles about removing dams and reams of photocopied scholarly studies about the Timbisha Shoshone. To look at the sheer volume of research they'd inspired, no one could say the tribe had been ignored, but the way they were revered in this esoteric academic world seemed at odds with the way they actually lived. My second stack of papers—small-town news articles and obscure blog postings—made that clear.

Trouble arose for the Timbisha almost as soon as the Homeland Act passed. The act permitted the tribe to acquire a specific property outside the park, the Lida Ranch, and a tiny loophole allowed that if not that property, another "suitable property" could be substituted. In the early 2000s, a developer swept onto the scene and proposed to the tribal council that through that loophole, the Timbisha might acquire land in Hesperia, a small California desert town to the south of Death Valley, not far from Palm Springs and halfway from Los Angeles to Las Vegas. The perfect place for a casino. The developer pushed, the Hesperia City Council resisted, and the Timbisha splintered into factions.

Truth is, the splintering had already begun. The tribal council changed hands rapid-fire during the early years. Even Pauline Esteves, the elder who had led the battle for the Homeland Act, lost her seat because of how she chose to distribute funds or because of personality conflicts or, some said, because of her propensity for doing business in her native tongue. Others moved in, people from the outside. On one hand, it made sense. Not all members of the tribe had chosen to stay put in Death Valley. Many lived elsewhere. To earmark funds for development projects at Furnace Creek seemed unfair to them. The Timbisha in the small towns of Bishop or Lone Pine, California—two hundred miles away from Death Valley— or those in, say, Cincinnati, two thousand miles away, would gladly take cash payments instead, and they would gladly take casino money, too. So would some of the Death Valley Indians, but the tribal council believed the proposal was shoddy, the developers shady. The deal fell through, but the hard feelings lingered.

Years passed. A new developer brought a new casino proposal, and when the sitting council rejected this one, too, the situation seriously deteriorated. Now, as best I could tell, a Timbisha man about my age named Joe Kennedy headed an unrecognized Death Valley–based council while, in Bishop, George Gholson held the official reins. I had tried repeatedly over the past months to contact Gholson. Phone calls. Emails. No reply. I tried to email Barbara Durham as she'd suggested. No reply. She was still listed as the official tribal historic preservation officer, a paid position that I hoped remained outside the political fray. Once, midwinter, I took a trip downlake on the ferry from phoneless Stehekin to spend two nights in a hotel just to try to talk to her. I left several messages on a machine, then finally one afternoon a woman answered.

As soon as I began to speak, she hung up.

Then in December an article in the *Los Angeles Times* reported that the state of California would stop providing bus service for a handful of kids to get from Furnace Creek to school in Death Valley Junction, sixty miles away. On a whim, I wrote to Barbara Durham to ask about this new development. This time she replied immediately. She told me the article had persuaded some anonymous person to lobby on their behalf. The busing had resumed. But that was the only good news. She laid out the rest of the story with more than a hint of exasperation. The casinos. The warring councils.

Our tribe has been caught in turmoil since the passage of the Timbisha Homeland Act due to gaming.

I reread the note now—she'd responded to none of my follow-ups—and stared out the window into the gray. I found contact information for Joe Kennedy and sent a note to him. It couldn't hurt. But I was not hopeful.

I reminded myself: theirs is not the only story. Right out the window, in fact, another was unfolding.

Tomales Bay, a narrow fifteen-mile inlet of the Pacific, stabs into the north coast of California at a steep southeast angle, and forms the east boundary of Point Reyes National Seashore. The hut where I worked sat directly above the southern tip. The small picturesque town of Inverness across the way slipped in and out of view, houses tucked in trees, trees tucked in the clouds; it could be Scotland, yes, or Juneau or the Olympic Peninsula. The bay is known largely for oyster production, but from here you could see no oyster beds, only the seabirds in constant motion, skittering all hours of the day, against a medley of dark green and dark gray and mud.

Each morning, I ran at dawn through spongy wet grass, along a trail populated by dairy cows and songbirds, toward marshlands and past a sign that read: Giacomini Wetland Restoration Project. Park Service brochures described the project. In the early part of the twentieth century, settlers built dikes and levees along Lagunitas Creek and its tributaries— the source of two-thirds of the Tomales Bay's freshwater—to protect roads and farms from flooding. Over time, these structures allowed sediment to build up and non-native species to move in, and water quality declined precipitously. So, in 2000, the National Park Service used money from congressional allocations and from the California Department of Transportation to acquire the 550-acre Waldo Giacomini Ranch, plus an additional thirteen acres of upland mesa.

Park employees and contractors and volunteers began work right away, removing non-native plants like Himalayan blackberry and eucalyptus, hauling out decades of manure, filling in drainage ditches, dismantling barns, bulldozing new tidal channels. Hopes ran high that the restored wetlands would work more efficiently than dikes as flood control, that more birds, ducks especially, and fish and amphibians—the endangered California red-legged frog, for one—would return, and that the water itself would be cleaner with fewer cows on the land, no septic systems feeding the bay, and native plants breaking down the bacteria. But there was also fear. Breach the levees and you could release trapped pesticide residue, excessive sediment, god knows what. In 2008, they breached the levees in front of five hundred cheering attendees, flooding 563 acres at a cost of $12 million. The dividend came fast. Water quality improved more dramatically in the first year than anyone had predicted.

I sat watching the shorebirds running across the flats again, like schoolkids at recess or confetti in the wind. Tomales Bay is one of the most biologically diverse areas in the United States, and the wildlife, by all accounts, was thriving in the wake of the breach. The project had been inarguably successful. But. The Department of Transportation had funded its portion of the project as a (mandated) way to mitigate for sins committed elsewhere. This kind of grand bargain is the lifeblood of restoration projects. Pave a wetland. Fund restoration. Kill off one species. Restore another. Was this a newfangled utilitarian version of reclaiming? Take back one place, make it right, in exchange for making another place useful? Or was it a perversion?

Maybe it was neither. Not all the money came from DOT or even from Congress. Much came from conservation groups, state and local governments, and private funders. If I held skepticism at bay, I could see this as a genuine non-species-centric many-stakeholders experiment.

This brought to mind the Mountain Maidu, Lorena Gorbet's tribe in the Sierras who had gathered so many stakeholders in order to take on the stewardship project with the Forest Service. How did that look from the bureaucrats' side? I called the Forest Service tribal liaison for the Maidu at his office in Quincy and left a message asking if he'd be available to talk. He returned my call saying he'd be glad to, but I'd have to send my questions in writing in advance. I headed out on a walk.

At the grocery store in the tourist town a few blocks away I stood in line and examined postcards of the nearby lighthouse and green rolling hills and one of an odd ungulate ghostly white in the mist. The creature was strange, mystical, nearly ridiculous. It may as well have been a jackalope. I read the back of the card: Tule Elk. Not pretend. I tossed the postcard in my basket—Laurie would have to see this to believe it— and laid my purchases on the counter: the postcard, four apples, two potatoes, and a chocolate bar. A twenty didn't cover the cost. I crossed the street. The Western Tavern was the only establishment that seemed less gentrified than the rest of town. The Pine Cone Diner came in a close second, but when one of the other writers went in for breakfast he'd been distressed to see overall-clad farmers reading the *New Yorker*. The board-and-batten front of the Western Tavern had weathered gray. The neon beer signs in the window lit thick dust. I was hopeful. But I began to wonder when I walked through the doors at four thirty on a Friday at the height of March Madness and found the place deserted. I pulled up a stool and ordered a six-dollar IPA from the local Lagunitas microbrewery. Before taking my money, the bartender, a woman, stuck out her hand to shake, something I'd never seen a bartender do, ever. A friendly gesture, I figured, but I didn't much want to chat. I wanted to watch basketball. Another patron walked in, another woman, and she and the bartender proceeded to get into a loud debate about where to buy or collect the best native seeds for landscaping.

My team lost. I finished my beer, left a tip, and walked back into the rain. They'd taken over, these sustainability-minded people—we had— taken this place back from the crusty working-class, male-centric culture. Why this kind of evolution continued to depress me, I couldn't say. Maybe as much as reclaiming is a human instinct, I thought, so is the instinct to experience change as loss.

A kind of despair encroached, the kind that seeps in when you're far from home and the sky stays gray for a week, and whatever project you're devoted to, from making bread dough to balancing the checkbook, seems doomed. I sat staring at my pile of paper and my collection of empty coffee mugs. The rain stopped, but clouds hung at eyebrow level.

I didn't know what else to do, so I called my mom. I wanted to catch up on news and to make plans for another road trip. I was in the same state; it seemed silly not to. The research did not seem to be panning out. And what mattered more anyway? We decided to meet at the Steinbeck museum—she and Laurie and I had been holding an informal long-distance book club reading his Monterey novels—and I wondered, too, would she want to go to Yosemite? A four-hour drive out of our way, but we could do a quick overnight. I'd never been and she'd never been. Mom was excited. She said she'd call the Auto Club, get some maps. I'd make motel reservations. I made a note on a pad and gazed down at the bay to where the shorebirds stood.

That's when I saw it, curled on an Adirondack chair not three feet from the window, the slender pointed nose, the tucked tail unmistakably bushy: the red fox.

He opened one eye and met my gaze warily, then closed it again.

"I gotta go, Mom," I said.

I scrambled for my camera, raised it to my eyes, and the fox was gone. I raced to the house, eager to share the news of my sighting, but the other writers were not around. Rain had started again and pinged into metal pails catching drips in the great room while I perused the books, which covered the wall floor to ceiling, books written by people who'd stayed at the retreat alongside the classic texts of nature writing, some on economics, many on politics.

One title caught my eye: *Tending the Wild: Native American Knowledge and the Management of California's Natural Resources* by M. Kat Anderson. I thumbed through absently, still thinking about the fox. Did the book mention the Maidu or the Timbisha? It did. It contained entire sections on how they lived with the land, how they used plants and animals, mostly how they had faith in renewal.

"The cultures of indigenous people of California," Anderson explained, "are rooted in a belief that nature has an inherent ability to renew itself, to cause the return of geese, the re-growth of the plants, the germination of next year's crop of wildflowers."

I sank into a chair to devour the book.

When I returned to my room after dark, emails from Joe Kennedy and Barbara Durham awaited. There was a council meeting planned, the alternative council, Joe's council, and I'd be welcome to attend.

On my last day in Marin, I went in search of the reclusive Tule elk. A sighting would be unlikely, but I was hopeful nonetheless since I'd already seen whales and elephant seals and a single red fox. I drove the winding road past dairy farms and barbed-wire fences, and finally a small sign for the Tule Elk Reserve, just past which I nearly smacked into a rented motor home parked on the center line. A man with a camera with a lens as long as my forearm stood shooting into the mist.

There they stood, not one but dozens, and they were exactly as they'd appeared on the postcard: white, ghostly, absurd, miraculous. When I read up on them I found that there'd been half a million in California when Europeans arrived, but the population had dwindled to twenty-eight in 1895. More than any other species I knew of, they were revived by a single individual, a Los Angeles schoolteacher named Beula Edmiston, who spent a decade lobbying for their protection. Today there are four thousand crowding the bucolic hillsides so thoroughly that the Park Service is trying to figure out ways to manage the population.

The story delighted me.

We live in an era of mass extinctions unknown since before humans walked the earth, extinctions we know are caused precisely because we walk the earth. There's no avoiding that hard fact or the associated hard grief or hard guilt, but there are these exceptions, species returned from the brink. Besides the gray whales and the elephant seals and the Tule elk, in my short lifetime I'd seen California condors, peregrine falcons, gray wolves, and Canada geese with my own eyes, all species that should've been gone before I arrived because of human behavior, all species that survived because some human made an effort, often a long and arduous effort, to save them. Ever since I'd started thinking about reclamation, I'd worried that I was being a Pollyanna, looking on the ridiculously unwarranted bright side. At Point Reyes, I realized it was not because I didn't know about the state of the earth that I was drawn to these stories, but because I did.

But they were rarely uncomplicated. Like the red fox. After my encounter, I talked to friends who convinced me the fox was my helpmate, that in Chinese mythology he often is. Certainly my mood and fortunes had improved when he appeared. A friend had sent me a black-and-white photo of her grandmother cradling a red fox, and every time I began to lose faith, I'd look at the photo. Hard to say if taming a fox is the right thing to do or the wrong, or just plain foolhardy, but I'm telling you: that woman looked powerful.

Later I'd learn that that the red fox does appear in mythology, but usually as a more cunning and malicious trickster than playful coyote. I'd learn that red foxes adjust well to urban environments, where they wreck gardens and spread disease, especially rabies, that they're considered an invasive species, especially in Australia, and that at least one conservation group keeps them on a list of species that are more or less okay to let slip into extinction.

I snapped photos of the elk and climbed into the Buick to continue my journey. I'd meet my mother first, then I'd be adrift. Joe Kennedy had changed the date of the council meeting, so my most recent plan—south to Death Valley, stop in with the Maidu on the way north—had been unrigged. Now I'd go north first, then south, then north again. As long as the Buick held together. I tried to call and reschedule with everyone.

No one was answering. Nothing to do but show up.

7

Tending

Quincy, California—March 2012

All day I followed the Feather River. The river churned in the canyon below, and hillsides rose in a lush tangle of chaparral and pine and oak, and at Belden Town a once-neon martini glass perched on an abandoned railroad bridge. The winding road passed a stately aging powerhouse, testament to the New Deal glory days of hydropower, and was pocked with construction and bridge reconstruction. Frequent oversized Forest Service signs reminded whoever might heed them that you need a permit to cut a tree. There were hardly any pullouts, and on a spring day, hardly any traffic. Still it was late afternoon before I reached Quincy, the Plumas County seat and the only town in the county with a chain grocery store, Safeway, or fast-food joint, Subway. This high-elevation former floodplain, now unimaginatively dubbed American Valley, was once Maidu country, but the last census found it 87 percent white, an astonishing majority for California, and only 1 percent Native American.

A light drizzle had begun, and white clouds settled in pockets in the soft conifer fringe on the hills, and nearly everything was shut down. So I checked into the Pine Hill Motel, cutesified log cabins on a wet highway-side lawn featuring picnic tables and bears made from pine rounds and at least a dozen American flags. When I checked in—the only guest for the night so far—the owner asked about my business in town.

"The Maidu? Lotta folks interested in that history," he said.

I settled into a room newly decorated for Easter with stuffed bunnies on every surface, switched on the baseboard heat, and started coffee. Since I'd changed plans so often, I doubted anyone would return my calls, but I'd just taken my first sip when the phone rang. Darrel Jury, a local environmental studies professor, wondered if I could meet him in five minutes. I could.

Feather River College sat right across the highway. By the time I'd finished my coffee and pulled on a light rain jacket, he and I were walking in darkening woods behind the modest college buildings. Students scurried past, leaving for the day, but Darrel, in well-worn boots and a clean canvas work coat, seemed in no hurry. He explained that the college came into existence only in 1970; before that it was a ranch and before that a Maidu village.

"See the blue flagging over there?" He pointed upslope toward a series of flat depressions, like staggered terraces, marked by blue ribbons tied to the rough, curled, finger-like limbs of small-diameter pines.

"Looks like tent pads."

"Those were Maidu summer home sites. There are about twenty of those on this hillside and others elsewhere."

Darrel traced the history with care as we walked a trail layered with the fall's detritus. Brown oak leaves and pine needles matted the ground a colorless in-between: no longer snowy, not yet green. The Maidu were forced off around the turn of the last century, and the understory burning that they'd done seasonally stopped cold. For four decades, every forest fire that started was suppressed until, predictably, the Big One came to devour all that unburned fuel. In 1946, several lightning-strike fires started, burned together, and killed off much of the surrounding forest completely.

He paused.

"Right," I said. Meaning: Go on.

I couldn't tell if his hesitation was born of a scientist's precision or a bureaucrat's caution or something else. He seemed naturally shy and exceedingly humble, nothing like my stereotype of an academic, even one in environmental science, but there was something else at work too, something I couldn't name.

He continued the story. The forest around the college, he explained, had grown back since '46, and like most of the forest in the area—he may as well have said in the American West—it'd grown too thick, too lush, again without suppression. Here at last Jury got to his point. He didn't want to see the pattern repeat itself: lightning strike and then devastation. He wanted to use the principles of traditional ecological knowledge to reintroduce fire. He'd received a grant to start a pilot program, and some work had already begun.

At the mention of TEK, his voice kicked up a half-octave, more animated, more excited. I asked what he knew about the history of the concept, when it came into acceptability.

"It's relatively recent," he said. "There's a woman. I have her book."

He struggled to remember the title. I pictured the volume I'd discovered on the shelf at the writers retreat a week earlier on the day I saw the red fox.

"Is it *Tending the Wild*?" I asked. "By M. Kat Anderson?"

He stopped in his tracks to turn and face me for the first time.

"Yes, yes."

I stood waiting for more.

"How did that book make a difference?"

He rocked on his boots, his hands balled in his jacket pockets.

"Well, in the sixties there was a romanticizing of the indigenous people."

This was not exactly news.

"But on the academic side, it wasn't until Kat Anderson that we began to see the California Indians are really unique with their agro-ecology practices. They don't fit the pigeonhole of either hunter-gatherers or agrarian. They managed the wild."

"Did you learn that in school?"

He shook his head. "*Tending the Wild* was for me a lot of epiphanies, a lot of new information."

"What did you believe before then?" I asked. "Where were you coming from?"

He used to work for the Forest Service, he said, then later for the Park Service, and for the Bureau of Land Management as a wilderness manager in Colorado.

"I guess I had more of a hands-off approach," he said.

He wasn't the only one.

There was a time when nearly everyone who came from college to work in the woods, as I did in my early twenties, was some version of a "Nashie," someone who'd studied Roderick Nash, the author of *Wilderness and the American Mind*. Nashies had a hardcore hands-off approach to wild lands. Flower sniffers, they were sometimes called, a step beyond tree huggers.

If I wasn't exactly a flower sniffer, it was hard not to side with them. You could see the stakes so clearly in the Pacific Northwest in the early 1990s, the short window between the Reagan era of unbridled clear-cutting and the closed-mill era when the endangered spotted owl brought it all to a halt. In those days, you could walk to work on a trail and see fresh slash—the trampled deciduous brush, discarded limbs, and too-small trees strewn or stacked in the wake of a clear-cut, looking like the aftermath of a tornado—for miles on one side of a wilderness boundary sign and seven-foot-diameter old-growth cedars on the other. Who wouldn't choose the cedars? The language of the 1964 Wilderness Act was seared into our minds and hearts: a place where man is only a visitor. The literature in the ranger station translated it to sound bites: *Take only pictures, leave only footprints*, or more succinctly: *Leave no trace*. Flower sniffing influenced everyone I worked with in some way, an entire subculture, albeit a small one, for whom wilderness was very nearly a religion.

Was. Over time, my faith began to erode. Work in the woods long enough and you learn at least two lessons. First, even with hand tools, you can get a lot more done than you think. Second, no matter how devastating the effects of that work may appear, they will fade. You can clear a ten-foot swath, and by the next season it'll look as though it's suffered years of neglect. Even native vegetation thrived despite, and sometimes in response to, our efforts; wildflowers flourished and short trees grew tall with new access to sunlight. Allow real years to add up, and for better or worse, you'd think humans had never touched the place. Of course, the Pacific Northwest is unique: not as dry as California or the Interior West and not even close to as dry as the Southwest. But the lesson was not so much about fecundity, or even fragility, as about habitation. The longer I worked, the more I realized: No way were we the first humans to work in this so-called wilderness. Which made me suspect that the scars we'd left were less damaging than the all-or-nothing philosophy we'd bought into.

The smell of new rain in the forest mixed with exhaust from heating vents from the college buildings behind us. We walked fast and talked slow, and the rhythm grew more comfortable. I began to suspect that I understood Darrel's habitual hesitation. The concept of tending can sound like blasphemy, like an excuse for more human meddling, to a true wilderness believer, even a former believer.

We came to a place where we could see a wall of trees just beyond the Maidu summer home sites, where oaks disappeared and pines grew in straight rows.

"It's interesting how priorities go. The Maidu valued oaks for the acorns; in fact they called them 'acorn trees,' but contemporary land managers valued the pines."

You could see the preference on the land as clear as in a community garden where one gardener chooses to grow only potatoes, while another plants peas, beans, tomatoes, squash, and beets. A whole different look. A whole different approach. The Maidu wouldn't have burned out all the pine—they prized it for the nuts—and they cultivated incense cedars, too, to use the bark for their houses. But oak was the mainstay.

"Some of the oaks survived the '46 fires," Darrel said. "With others, the fires killed the main stems but the roots survived and stump-sprouted."

The college hired a local all-Indian fire crew, mostly Maidu, from the Greenville Rancheria, he said, and part of the work they did was to thin stump-sprouted stems back to a few leaders, to get them to grow larger and produce more acorns. But the bulk of their work had been pile burning. That's all they could safely manage, at least until the fuel load gets reduced enough by thinning to allow small-scale broadcast burns like the ones the Maidu set in the past. Still, Darrel hoped that would happen sooner than later.

"In this oak woodland, some plots will burn annually, some every two years, others every three years, and then we'll look at how fire influences vegetation, probably work with traditional practices of . . . well, we'll see what comes up."

If there's bear grass, for example, which was a staple for basketry, they'd try to maintain that. Elsewhere, in a more riparian zone, they might manage for willow. There's a greenhouse on campus at the college, and he hoped to have students collect seeds or cuttings and cultivate plants there. They were working with Trina Cunningham, a local Maidu woman.

"Is she related to Farrell Cunningham?"

"That's her brother," he said.

I'd been intrigued by Farrell Cunningham, the young president of the Maidu Summit Consortium, ever since hearing about him from Lorena Gorbet. I'd read plans he wrote for using TEK on private trust lands, and I'd been struck, over and over, by the way he combined the scientific and the humanistic, the practical and the spiritual.

"The meadow and surrounding ecosystem will be re-invigorated," he wrote in one project description, "through a combination of thinning, pruning, seeding, burning, traditional resource procurement methods, singing, talking, and prayer." Singing, talking, and prayer? Guiding principles included these: "Humans are part of the ecosystem. All other ecosystem components are people too."

I wanted to understand, but didn't quite.

"How will Trina be involved?" I asked Darrel.

"She'll help us develop a management plan that integrates TEK and provides some . . . well, how do I say it? Traditional wisdom has been downplayed, not acknowledged. Some of the wisdom has been co-opted . . ." The sentence dangled.

He wanted to talk about it, but he didn't quite know how.

We walked in silence, then, along the narrow trail. Mule deer lay in shallow depressions, chewing lazily. You could see we'd interrupted them, and they rose from their beds reluctantly. The drizzle had grown into full-fledged rain, which pattered loudly on the oak leaves in the dirt. Darrel and I moved inside to a book-crowded office, where I quickly scanned the shelves like a nosy houseguest craving camaraderie in a vinyl copy of *Abbey Road* or a dog-eared *Our Bodies Ourselves* or a leather-bound King James Bible. There it was: *Wilderness and the American Mind.*

Wilderness, Nash argues, is an ideal more than a physical location. His book traces the idea from the Old Testament, through writers like Thoreau, Muir, and Leopold, with nods to other cultural figures like painter Thomas Moran and landscape architect Frederick Law Olmstead; even Forest Service founder Gifford Pinchot makes a cameo as the bad guy who sided with wise use rather than preservation. If the fact that these thinkers are all men, all white, nearly all Ivy League graduates rankles—and it does—it's important to remember the book first appeared in 1967, before political correctness had saturated academia.

Not just political correctness. Data. Research. Facts. Archaeological evidence has accrued for three decades—documented in new editions of natural history guides like *California Indians and Their Environment* and popularized more broadly in books like Charles Mann's *1491*—to show that the central defining characteristic of wilderness as "a place untouched by humans" is largely false, at least if you take "untouched" to mean "has never been manipulated." Humans inhabited many now-protected landscapes for centuries, and they shaped nature to suit their needs. Besides planting and cultivating, they set fires to improve habitat for game, then hunted, and sometimes overhunted. The problem, in other words, isn't just that *Wilderness and the American Mind* is too patriarchal or too extreme, the problem is that the concept itself is naïve at best, or maybe plain wrong.

Tending the Wild may never have the reach of *Wilderness and the American Mind.* Maybe because its scope is not as broad—Anderson's focus is strictly on the California tribes—or maybe because it's not as ideological. Anderson's research is thorough and complex and precise. The 526-page tome contains 45 pages of notes, another 60 of small-print bibliography, and 50 of index. Sometimes she gleans knowledge from anthropologists' writings, but more often she learns from the Indians

Ana Maria Spagna   79 themselves, and she includes specific examples from over three dozen tribes. One chapter alone contains references to texts ranging in publication date from 1877 to 1996, plus personal interviews with tribal elders. It is undeniably exhaustive, but it's neither a manifesto nor a how-to guide. There is something about *Tending the Wild* that feels modest. Maybe because what it espouses is, essentially, a modest practice.

"To both use and conserve nature requires complex knowledge and practices, far more complex than leaving nature alone," Anderson argues.

She describes dozens of practices from the Maidu alone. When digging ponderosa roots for basketry materials, for example, they'd take the roots from one side of the tree one year, and the other side the next. They harvested alder bark for dyes without felling or girdling the trees. They limited the gathering of roots and bulbs of wild carrot and camas to allow them to resprout the next year. They pinched off leaves of tobacco to smoke in stone pipes but left the stalk to mature so the seeds could be replanted the next year.

"An overarching gathering rule was to spare plants and plant parts; do not harvest everything," she explains.

This may sound to a backyard gardener like plain common sense, but the repercussions loom large. Some environmentalists, even researchers who admire Anderson, worry that a new movement is afoot to supplant the myth of the wilderness with the myth of the humanized landscape, and it worries them. Proving wilderness never existed could become an excuse to exploit it. I was aware of the danger. I didn't want to be reactionary. I also feared—how do you say this gently?—that white people don't do modesty when it comes to nature. The image of that stark line of the clear-cut against the wilderness boundary stuck in my mind. We're an all-or-nothing society with heavy emphasis on the all. Blame capitalism or Judeo-Christian teachings or, in the case of most non–Native Americans, plain un-rootedness. If you don't stay long enough to have a connection with a place, you may see no danger in, say, harvesting every last seed. (Not that staying assures you'll be modest either, but local knowledge is at the root of *Tending the Wild*.)

Still, wholesale ideological flip-flopping is not Anderson's point. Her point is, in some ways, more radical. Anderson believes the old ways might be a bulwark against the future, that tending might be a way to save threatened native plants, to allow them to thrive. This answered one of my shameful lurking questions. Why bother? Isn't practicing the old ways nothing more than historic reenactment, like dressing up like Yanks and Rebs, a sometimes unsettling mix of nostalgia and fantasy? No, Anderson argues, traditional knowledge has a practical purpose: in an era of shrinking natural resources, we can save what's left by learning how to tend it.

The sky had grown dark, and Darrel checked his watch often. His wife was coming to pick him up any minute. Headlights strobe-lit a parking lot in a meadow off the highway as students left campus for the day. They're local kids, Darrel explained when I asked about them, a few Maidu students, but not many. Most are mountain kids who love the outdoors, so the school has a large environmental studies program and a highly ranked rodeo team. I wondered if they came in knowing anything at all about California Indians.

"Probably not. You know, most Californians think that Natives are all dead."

That, I suspected, was about right. I remembered the clerk at the motel saying people are interested in "that history."

I couldn't help thinking that Darrel Jury's students were lucky. They'd see the land and Native people through his eyes, they'd learn a different way; they might even learn to practice TEK the way my generation learned to protect wilderness. I landed back with the Easter bunnies at the Pine Tree Motel and found two messages waiting: one from Maidu elder Beverly Ogle confirming my visit to her home down in Paynes Creek—ninety miles back over the pass the way I'd come—the next afternoon and a second from Wade McMaster, the Forest Service–tribal liaison, who said he could meet me for lunch. I returned his call and asked if he thought I could meet him and still make it to Beverly's.

"If you leave early," he said, "and don't hit too much snow."

I rose early to jog along the river. As dawn began to brighten rain-wet pines you could see why the Sierras are the Range of Light, why California is the Golden State. I gazed out at American Valley and tried to picture it as it once was, before Safeway or Subway, before the wet meadows full of beavers were drained for cattle and hay, before the Maidu were reduced to 1 percent of the human population. I couldn't. I walked on the highway shoulder until pavement-reflected sunlight blinded me completely, and then I stopped in my tracks thinking this: Maybe reclaiming isn't about how it used to be or even how it should be, but how it could be.

8

Without an Invite

Paynes Creek, California—March 2012

From Quincy I drove south through Greenville, nestled, as the name suggests, in deep green forest, the road lined with trailer homes and power lines, an auto wrecker and a sheriff's office with a faux western front, a high school marquee that read "Home of the Indians: Booster club meeting Wednesday." Just outside of town, the road began to climb and snow began to fall. Large yellow highway signs and scratchy radio announcements warned that tire chains were required, but I continued on, chainless, over a high mountain pass, then down. I was alone in the Buick, downshifting into third then second, my tire tracks in the rearview mirror the only scars on a thick wet skim of snow until, at four thousand feet, the snow gave way to rain and a hard wind picked up in the rolling hills of the Sacramento River Valley. Six egrets sat in a field, wings tucked in tight as the wind blew hard through a barbed-wire fence. What, I wondered, could they possibly be doing out there so exposed?

Wade McMaster had suggested we meet at a roadside diner, but when I showed up at the lone wooden structure—the only establishment for miles amidst rain-soaked farmlands and forest—I found the doors locked, the windows shuttered. A large white Chevy Suburban pulled into the lot, and the driver—Wade McMaster presumably—

motioned with one arm out the window for me to follow him down-valley toward Highway 99, the inland north-south route at the base of the foothills of the Sierras, the working-class route. Traffic raced both directions midday, midweek, as we pulled into the strip mall parking lot of Two Buds BBQ.

When Wade McMaster stepped out of the Suburban, I had to mask my surprise. The forty-three-year-old Wintu tribal chairperson and the Forest Service tribal liaison for the Plumas and Lassen National Forests had blue eyes and short sandy hair. He wore a flannel shirt over an immaculate white T-shirt and two earrings in one ear, and he sported tattoos on his forearms. He looked part hipster, part redneck, and not one bit Indian. While we stood in line to order tri-tip sandwiches, I brought up the fact that his bosses had requested that I send my questions for him ahead, via email, so they could be vetted in D.C.

"Washington D.C. Seriously?" I asked

"Seriously," he said with an agreeable shrug.

What had seemed to me a grievous wrong, a clear encroachment on First Amendment rights, was to him just another hoop to jump through in a never-ending series of hoops.

We sat at a table mid-room under bright fluorescent lights and began to chat as AM radio played contemporary country music and the other BBQ patrons, mostly older white men, strained to overhear our conversation. I tried to ask about the Maidu stewardship program with the Forest Service, but it quickly became clear that before he could even begin to talk about that, or anything related to his job, I'd need a basic primer on Indian divisions in California. Darrel Jury had mentioned a fire crew from the Greenville Rancheria.

"What exactly is a rancheria?" I asked. "Like a mission?"

"Sort of," he said. And he was off.

Change happened fast in California, and the gold rush trumped everything. Sometimes there was no time for treaties and often any treaties that were written were voided in Washington D.C. The land was too valuable, the Indians too easily expendable, and as a result, they were chased off over and over again, so often, to so many places, that they had no place left. So in the early 1900s, in an act of either compassion or contrition or both, Congress allocated land to serve as rancherias, small plots, maybe thirty to forty acres, fifty of them in the state, which would become, essentially, homeless shelters.

"You didn't have to be a specific tribe. A lot of people wonder why a rancheria has a lot of different tribes on it. That's why."

His blue-eyed gaze grew more intense.

"Then as part of termination, the rancherias were broken up, disbanded."

Termination. The word carries a sinister connotation in any context. You can terminate a job, an insurance policy, even a life. In Indian history, the word conjures an era not long ago, the early 1950s, when Congress passed a series of laws designed to get all Indians off the federal dole and make them regular tax-paying Americans. Reservations were to be broken up, land would be sold to the highest bidders, and Indians would be assimilated. The irony lay in the result. The American Indian Movement rose up in opposition to termination, and it moved fast. Astonishingly so. Less than twenty years later, land in California was returned to descendants of rancheria residents with full federal recognition. The result is that you have federally recognized entities, sovereign nations in effect, that aren't all one tribe, and you also have more homogeneous tribes—like McMaster's own tribe, the Wintu—that can't get recognized. They've been trying for thirty years. They're trying still.

He paused to see if I was with him so far and to take a first bite of his sandwich. I saw his eyes flick toward the counter, but the old white guys had lost interest.

"It's all about relationships," he said. "That's why the Mountain Maidu have been so successful." He cited the Maidu Summit Consortium, the nonprofit Lorena Gorbet had told me about, the one composed of unincorporated community groups, federally recognized rancherias, and petitioning aboriginal tribal governments (Greenville Rancheria, Roundhouse Council Indian Education Center, Mountain Maidu Preservation Association, Susanville Indian Rancheria, Maiduk We'ye, Tasmam Koyom Cultural Foundation, Tsi-akim Maidu, United Maidu

Nation, and the Maidu Culture & Development Group). "I wouldn't mind modeling something like that in our Wintu tribe," he said.

Wade McMaster has the ideal personality for a liaison. He grew up in small mountain towns knowing little about his ancestry, went to junior college, tried to find work, and when he had no luck, joined the Air Force. Only when he got home from overseas did he begin to get more interested in his heritage. He started attending tribal council meetings and language classes. He also finished a degree in counseling and took up songwriting. My initial impression—part redneck, part hipster—was not far off the mark, I discovered, but you'd have to add military veteran and therapist to the mix.

He came around at last to the stewardship project. He explained how the Maidu were trying to practice traditional ecological knowledge while also trying to teach the concepts to Forest Service officials and how, for a long while, things weren't going well.

"You have to understand you had two different cultures, the culture of the government agency that deals with strict contracting and regulations, rules, policies, then tribes that are more fluid in whatever they do. Some of the things the tribe was doing were not fitting in."

That much I'd heard from Lorena Gorbet months before, but this I had not: the project was more or less stagnant when the fire crew from Greenville Rancheria came on the scene.

"They were young, fired up," he said.

Not inconsequentially, they were also willing to work for cheap. They were led by a young guy named Danny Manning, who had experience in wildland firefighting, and everyone on the crew was Native, though not all Maidu, and that made a difference in a thousand small ways. They could, for example, take the time to cut the trees they culled during thinning into firewood lengths and leave them for tribal elders, and sometimes elders would show up while they were working and tell stories—about how, say, this particular gooseberry bush belonged to this particular family, how they'd been using it for years—and the crew would listen.

Wade McMaster, despite his Forest Service job, did not overstate or whitewash. Was the project changing the lives of the young people working on Manning's crew? Probably not. The work was seasonal and low-paying, though Manning would later tell me that he can keep the crew working most of the year by burning piles in the winter, and at any rate, it's a job they might not otherwise have. But, he insisted, the stewardship project was making a difference.

"I'll give you an example," he said.

There was a broadcast burn planned with the goal of encouraging the native bear grass that was once used, and could be used again, as basketry material. Instead of using drip torches—the metal canisters filled with diesel and gas that would normally be used to start a prescribed burn—the Maidu wanted the crew to try to use pine boughs, to do it the traditional way. So you had these guys in their yellow Nomex firefighting gear carrying around pine boughs while the elders stood by and prayed. They tried and tried to get the fire going, but had no luck. The pine needles would burn out before the grass caught. Eventually, the guys got down on their hands and knees and crawled around using hand lighters to start the grass. No pine boughs, but no diesel either.

He stopped speaking and looked down at his plate, then pushed it away. Though we'd sat for over an hour it was clear he'd never finish his sandwich. He smiled a little and tipped his head boyishly.

"That just never would've happened before," he said. "Never."

Paynes Creek sat below the highway cutbank, just out of sight. The number of highway signs leading there would suggest it's a decent-sized town, but once you drop down to the small creek and follow the arcing curve of the single-lane road, you may wonder if the place exists at all. I drove past horses huddled under sheds and a single elementary school, flat-roofed, nondescript, but there was no sign of human life at all until, in the center of town, Beverly Ogle's farmhouse came into view: two-story, white, and modestly regal, with yellow lights in the windows and smoke from the chimney.

I pulled into the dirt driveway behind a white Ford Windstar van and tried to enter through a chain-link gate by pushing hard the wrong direction over thick green sod before realizing it needed to be pulled. When I looked up I saw Beverly peeking out the window from behind a curtain, watching me navigate, smiling without guile. She waved me in.

"Where would you like to sit?" she asked.

I gazed around the room. Every available surface was taken with books and photos and notebooks, the familiar paper-piled decor of an insatiable learner. Beverly Ogle is an author and an activist, a descendant of Atsugewi Pit River and Mountain Maidu and German Dutch people. Her two books, *Spirits of Black Rock* and *Whisper of the Maidu*, meld Native history and settler history and memoir with humor and precision. She leads courses for the Sierra Institute and speaks at conferences and is the vice-president of the Maidu Summit Consortium. She's seventy-one years old and apparently tireless.

"Maybe the kitchen," she said.

She moved slowly, cane in hand, through the front room, apologizing that with the woodstove, the living room must get over-hot in order to make the kitchen comfortably warm. When we reached the kitchen, she sat and crossed her arms. She wore her long dark hair streaked with gray pulled back and lofted over her head, and crow's-feet stemmed from the corners of her deep-set blue eyes. She wore a short-sleeved denim shirt that exposed her strong forearms. She also wore lipstick.

When I asked, she began to talk about Humbug Valley, how her ancestors lived there for generations until around 1860, when the place was flooded with gold miners and pioneers, and the Indian people retreated, hoping the whites would just move on through.

"When they saw that wasn't happening, they saw the inevitable, so they more or less accepted that and tried to become friends."

Her matter-of-fact conclusion surprised me, considering the magnitude of the loss. They were good people, really, these early settlers, Beverly insisted. Her great-grandfather had been angry at first, but later he worked for whites regularly: he cut cedar shakes, killed bears, and rendered lard to grease sled runners. He taught them how to live in that snowbound mountain country, how to snowshoe and shovel and trap. There was no hostility on either side. Not the way Grandma Benner told it, the grandmother with whom Beverly lived throughout childhood.

"I haven't come very far in life," Beverly said with a laugh. "Our home was probably about thirty miles back up this road." She gestured with one thumb over her shoulder.

The family had left Humbug Valley by then, and lived in Mill Creek—sixty miles west of Humbug and three thousand feet lower—where less snow fell, hardly any, and fruit trees flourished. I pictured their home to be much like this one in Paynes Creek, though in photos on Beverly's wall, it appeared more rustic, the land around it more wild, and it was not in the center of any town, however small.

Turned out I was one in a long line of outsiders Beverly's family had welcomed into their home over the years for the sake of preserving heritage. The most prominent was a linguist from UC Santa Cruz, William Shipley, who worked with Grandma Benner and with Beverly's mother, Maym Gallagher, to put together a dictionary of that Maidu language, and later—in a leapfrog of generations that nevertheless delights Beverly—passed the language down to Beverly's youngest son, Ken Holbrook. There had been a professional photographer, too, who took those photos of the Mill Creek homestead and made portraits of Grandma Benner: a smaller woman than Beverly, her skin darker, her gaze more skeptical, even through the lens of time, with an unmistakable glint of devilish humor.

As a kid, Beverly used to travel to Humbug Valley with Grandma Benner and her friends in an old Buick Roadmaster. Sometimes the old ladies let her drive even though she was only ten or eleven—this was the early 1950s after all—and she could hardly see over the hood. She drove high into the mountains while the elders gossiped in Maidu until the forest opened on a wide meadow where timothy grass and wild rye waved in the wind. The ladies taught Beverly how to gather the riches of the valley, like willows for basketry and ginger root for medicine. Grandma Benner also taught her there are no rattlesnakes in Humbug Valley. Go five miles one way or five miles another and you've got rattlesnakes. In Humbug Valley: none.

"It's because of that, and the natural soda springs up there, our Maidu people love Humbug Valley and believe it was a gifted place," Beverly said.

Changes came hard in the Feather River basin: more mining, more railroads, more dams. Most of it bypassed Humbug Valley, but by the early 1950s, things were changing even there: the campground was built, and tourists swarmed in. I asked if there was heartbreak in it for her grandmother, and she insisted there wasn't, that Grandma Benner generally accepted things, kept her feelings to herself, and moved on. Grandma Benner's photo, the face creased with deep-lined skepticism, belied that some. Maybe not heartbreak, but not resignation either.

When, late in life, Beverly Ogle took a job as campground host in Humbug Valley, she saw plenty of misbehavior: loud and drunk campers, off-highway vehicle riders who zipped through the meadows and tore up vegetation. She worked with PG&E to have a fence constructed to keep grazing cattle from tromping on Maidu graves. She hauled water to put out abandoned campfires. Mostly she talked. When people heard she was Maidu and that her family had history in the valley, they'd hit her with a familiar barrage of questions. But she didn't mind. She loved the place, and she loved the job.

Then came the day, in 2003, in the wake of the bankruptcy settlement, when PG&E representatives showed up in Humbug Valley to discuss potential new owners. "Stewards," they'd be called, since a conservation easement would accompany the title transfer. They'd invited a dozen or more officials from government agencies and nonprofits to attend—but not the Maidu. Lorena Gorbet had told me how she and Beverly Ogle and Farrell Cunningham showed up anyway.

"Yes, we sneaked in," Beverly said with a chuckle. "I was working out there. I heard there was gonna be this meeting—all these big people—and I called Lorena and said: 'Did you hear? Did you know?' She said, 'No, but we'll crash the party.'"

"They must've been surprised to see you," I said.

"They were," she said.

But her concerns at first were more practical than political; she was less worried at that point about the title to the land than about the condition of the land.

"When we got there, Fish and Game officials were talking about this red-legged frog."

Her voice rose with incredulity.

"And here I'd been there all summer seeing all this destruction. So I told the Forest Service and PG&E and everyone there: If you don't come out and patrol and know what's going on, you won't have to worry about that old red-legged frog, this'll all go up in smoke."

The Maidu met only briefly that day with the powers that be, but it was a beginning.

"We started having our own meetings, getting the pamphlets. There was a lot that went on before we really got included."

Much of that work had to be done through the Maidu Summit. When they started out, they figured the consortium would help them get some things done: protecting gravesites, opposing new mining operations. Now, they had a chance to reclaim Humbug Valley.

"We had to be all pulling in the right direction," Beverly Ogle said, sitting in her warm kitchen while rain poured down the windowpanes. "Like the old saying goes: You take two twigs, you can bust them, but you put a bunch together, it's harder to bust."

The two books Beverly Ogle has written brim with adaptable characters who defy stereotypes. Her great-grandfather, a gold-mining Maidu teetotaler, fathered more than twenty children with two wives, including Ogle's great-grandmother, a Pit River Atugewsi woman whom he bought as a child at a slave auction. Ogle's mother played the violin and was shunned at her Indian school for having a white father; she later worked for a time as a fire lookout for the Forest Service. Ogle's uncles trapped otters, minks, ermines, beavers, bobcats, coyotes, and foxes, some into the 1980s. Her extended family includes loggers, miners, and employees of the power companies, as well as victims of the same companies, and activists, like herself, fighting against them.

In person, too, her stories began this way, with a broad swath of characters like those in a Larry McMurtry novel, but as time moved on and the heat from the woodstove in the living room seeped into the kitchen, she became less scripted, more pointed, with an edge of anger. Her arms were no longer crossed, her elbows rested wearily on the table. If I intervened to encourage her, to suggest a direction for her thoughts—a bad character tic—she'd correct me straightaway, and carry on.

Her next book, the one she insists will be her last, will be about the Indian boarding schools, the off-reservation schools where Indian children were sent for much of the twentieth century, often against the family's wishes—"kidnapped," Beverly says plainly—where they were stripped of language, culture, and belief systems and subjected to a military-like regimen and sometimes, too often, to outright abuse. As a child, Beverly collected stories—"horrendous stories," she says—from her elders, sitting quietly while the adults talked, writing often with a carpenter's pencil on scraps of cardboard boxes. She wasn't the best speller, and sometimes the adults were speaking Maidu and she tried to spell it phonetically. Her notes are hard to decipher, but she is trying. The story, tragic as it is, has to be told. Early in our conversation, when she was describing the Maidu Summit, she told me there was a time when the different Indian groups used to fight with one another.

"Well, that's just human nature," I said.

"It's much more than that," Beverly replied, shaking her head emphatically. "We were taught to be this way from the start at the darned Indian schools that taught us to be ashamed of who we were."

Like most Americans, I'd barely known about the boarding schools most of my life, even though one of the biggest in California—Sherman Indian Institute—was located in Riverside, my hometown. We ran cross-country meets against Sherman and lost every time, which only reinforced stereotypes, and that's pretty much all I knew. Once I began to learn more, I'd felt the same shock and shame that I'd felt visiting Manzanar, and my mother's admonishment echoed in my mind: never again.

Still, more than occasionally, once I began to pay attention, I'd heard people talk disparagingly about how Indians use the boarding school experiences as an excuse. Why keep talking about the past? These conversations always had a hard edge of exasperation and blame. By now, the naysayers suggest, Indians are more or less assimilated, for better or worse. It's hard even to tell who's Indian and who's not. Wade McMaster acknowledged as much when he admitted he hardly ever faces discrimination since he's the "whitest Indian you'll ever meet." I considered asking Beverly Ogle about that, but she'd already read my mind.

"The big difference between then and now, even though our skin is lighter—many of our Maidu people have green eyes, blue eyes, and the blood has dwindled in degree of Indian—the thing is we're still here, and we have an education, and we stand up for our rights."

The kitchen, by then, had grown nearly hot. I had tried to keep up with her, but couldn't. She's proud of her history with all of its complexities; she's bluntly honest and nostalgic and entertaining, but she is unequivocal when it comes to injustice. I was humbled by her righteous indignation. I'd felt it before in the South when talking to veterans of the civil rights movement. Now I felt it again. Only in this case, the stories always came back to place, or more precisely, to specific places. One in particular.

Even once the Maidu were allowed to enter the land discussions with PG&E, most of the focus remained on several parcels in a more developed area near Lake Almanor and the small mountain town of Chester. The Maidu were interested in these parcels, of course; like the Timbisha and the Wintu and many other tribes, they'd like to locate a cultural center, a museum, a gallery somewhere near a tourist mecca, and Lake Almanor, a destination for summertime boaters and fishermen, fits the bill. But it's Humbug Valley that means the most to Beverly Ogle. You can tell by the way she writes of the place in specific detail. She recounts how the Maidu harvested edible plants: the wild potatoes no bigger than a peanut, the berries—elderberry, thimbleberry, gooseberry, huckleberry—the wild currant and the wild plum and the peppermint that makes a fine stimulating tea, and how they burned off the willows along Yellow Creek to grow tender new shoots for basketry, and how they made their clothes of rabbit fur and buckskin. You can tell most of all by the way she drops her voice, the way her tone changes from outrage to excitement, when she describes the gatherings in the valley, the sacred bear dance that Farrell Cunningham would lead each year.

"Those events are so good for our Maidu people."

Our Maidu people. Never without the possessive. Never singular.

When it came time to leave, I jogged back outside jacketless in the wind-driven rain to get a baggie of home-dried apples, a meager gift from the north. The sky had darkened with the edge of dusk. I offered her the apples, and Beverly thanked me and asked if we also grow cherries. I said we did and that I'd send some in early summer. She said she'd send gooseberries. Did we have those? she asked. No, I said. So it'd make a good trade. We shook on it.

Leaving, I drove into rain that would not let up. I headed back toward the mountains and passed the egrets still standing like sentries, tucked in and exposed in the exact same place, their feathers ruffling madly in the wind, their legs seeming too spindly to hold them up. They must've had eggs, I figured, must have been protecting something precious. What other explanation could there be? What else is there, ever, to do?

9

The Circle of Life

Death Valley, California—March 2012

For months I'd harbored a fantasy of sleeping tentless under the stars in Death Valley, but right away I could see I'd need the tent, not so much for weather as for privacy, since a twelve-dollar site at Texas Spring Campground was about the size of a parking spot at Target. So I set it up and hiked a sandy ridge with a bag of Fritos and a can of bean dip and a warm can of Coors Light—the best meal available at the gas station mini-mart back in Beatty—to a high point to watch sunset seep pink across the sky, to feel the steady wind beating sand against my shins. I gazed out at the Furnace Creek mesquite groves. The first glimpse of green on any tree, any time, can be breathtaking, but there was something unique about the green of those mesquites—like a lime popsicle, the same brightness, nearly artificial—against the stark desert backdrop. As dusk turned to dark I reread the section in *Tending the Wild* about traditional methods of harvesting and processing mesquite beans. I'd wondered, in the past, how much nutrition a person could really get from those beans. More than Fritos and Coors Light. That much was for sure. The book described Timbisha pruning back the honey mesquite to prevent the lower branches and undergrowth from catching sand that would bury the trees—bury them whole—then harvesting the pods and roasting them in pits. The stories hold more weight when you're sitting alone in the sand in such a seemingly unfertile place.

Seemingly. Earlier in the day I'd stopped at the newly renovated visitor center in Furnace Creek where a brand-new movie theater, like theaters at most national parks, shows the same flick over and over: a scenery-rich overview with a dramatic score that attempts to argue, in twenty minutes, why the place matters. There's history, geology, botany, poetry, a Ken Burns–style photographic montage, and most surprisingly, there's historian Barbara Durham and the eighty-nine-year-old elder activist Pauline Esteves, larger than life, telling the story of their homeland in their own words. To start with, Barbara Durham says the Timbisha do not call it "Death Valley" because—duh—it's not dead, it's alive.

On that spring afternoon, the visitor center had indeed been alive, packed and buzzing with bikers in tight shorts, little kids with oversized sunglasses, European women in heels, all of them filling water bottles, paging through guidebooks, looking for the restrooms. Now I returned to my tent to find the night as alive as the day with snorers and gigglers and an exasperated mother alone with a whiny son in the tent next door.

"A lot of people say when they come here this feeling comes over them of being taken care of, that their body and soul are being healed," Barbara Durham said in the visitor center movie.

Under the not-visible stars with my iPod on loud and the human night sounds even louder, I lay awake thinking how I did not feel taken care of. I did not feel healed. I felt instead the familiar tired yearning of everyone looking for *something*, something natural or spiritual or cultural or maybe just sunshine in spring. We'd all crowded into the same place in part for the natural beauty, in part because of the validation of the label "national park." And what exactly did I want anyway? A righteous path to follow? Or just a noble ending to the Homeland Act saga, a story I'd clung to like a rope then traced to this junction of worn, ragged threads, unsure which to follow? Awake in my tent, I knew exactly what I wanted. I wanted to go home.

I had reason to be discouraged. From Maidu country, I'd driven south, through Reno and into the desert where green sage gave way to yellow sage, and cloud shadows skimmed over mountains exposed to their essence—ridges and knobs like elbows half-bent or reclining human silhouettes, faces to the sky—and the soft brown suede, like fur, across the land. I was in a hurry. I had a plan to meet with Joe Kennedy's alternative tribal council, and one day before that—first thing in the morning—a plan to meet with Barbara Durham, a meeting that had taken nearly five months to schedule. Traffic moved fast, but when it wasn't fast enough, I eased toward the yellow line and gunned it to pass, and once found myself speeding head-on toward a bicyclist hauling a trailer on the road shoulder who raised his arm high in salute. With his middle finger. Not a good omen.

I arrived in Beatty near sunset and just as I slowed for the turnoff into Death Valley, a sick thud sounded under the hood of the Buick. The power steering failed; the battery light flashed. I backtracked to the biggest gas station in town and asked the clerk restocking toffee peanuts if there was anyone who could help.

"Sure," he said and flipped open his phone. "John the Mechanic."

John the Mechanic arrived, red-faced and mustache-trimmed, and approached me where I stood beside the Buick with its hood up, staring into blinding afternoon sun. I began to describe the problem and offered him the keys so he could test-drive the car to see for himself.

"No goddamned need for that," he said, cigarette dangling from his lip, and reached down to pull a shredded belt from under the hood.

Could he replace it?

He shrugged.

"Depends. Might find one in town—thank Christ it's American—or I might have to drive to Vegas to get one."

"Probably no chance I'll make it to an interview tomorrow morning at eight?"

He shook his head and stubbed a butt under his boot toe.

"No goddamned way. Who do you need to talk to?"

"The Timbisha Shoshone down there in the park."

"The Indians?" John the Mechanic stared at me with an unreadable heavy-lidded gaze. "They're all drunks, you know, alcoholics. Very sad.

Some people can't handle it. Like me, I'm part Indian. Kind of people, one beer's not enough, two's too goddamned many."

"I'm sorry to hear that."

"And the Shoshones, they don't live down there, not all the time. Who the hell could live down there all the time?"

I shrugged. I had nothing to say to that. I needed my belt repaired.

"Will you take cash?" I asked.

"Only goddamned way I do business."

I called Barbara Durham and canceled our morning interview.

"No problem," she said. "Just call when you get down here."

I rented the cheapest room I could find—in a shabby dark-paneled motel dubbed the Atomic Inn in honor of the nearby test site—and late the next morning John the Mechanic called to give me the old good news/bad news routine. The good news was that my belt was fixed; the bad news was that my water pump was shot. I'd have to stop back in to have him fix it after a night in the park. Okay. Okay. Whatever. I was just glad he got me on the road. I drove fast, reached Furnace Creek by noon, radiator steaming, and called Barbara Durham from the visitor center parking lot. She answered on the first ring.

She couldn't meet me today after all.

"Tomorrow. 8:00. At the coffee shop," she said.

At night in the tent, I shut off the iPod. The battery was dying, and there was no place on the spectrum of neo-soul to alt-country to retro-punk that could offer comfort anyway. The wind had picked up, and my neighbors had drifted off to sleep, and as I pulled down the rain fly to gaze up through bug netting at more stars than I'd ever seen, I began to weep out of frustration and not-enough-dinner, and probably, more than anything, because I felt like an encroacher.

Pauline Esteves had addressed that feeling in the visitor center movie. "I've had some people say that when they look down here onto the valley floor they feel like they're interfering and they ask me if I feel that way, and I say if I wasn't connecting I will ask to be acknowledged and I will speak out to the Creator to be accepted."

When I heard it, I took this to mean she wanted to be acknowledged, yes, yes, and that's what I wanted, too—for her to be acknowledged, for her people to be justly recognized—but she was saying something else, something that made sense to me only in the incongruous crowded campground night, something about how an outsider should enter a new place: by acknowledging it's not your own, by asking to be accepted.

At first light, I took down the tent, packed it in the trunk, and drove a quarter mile to the Furnace Creek café an hour early to pace empty parking lots where maintenance workers hosed down asphalt and mourning doves cooed. Here in the uncrowded morning, I could examine the mesquite trees up close. I cradled a drooping blossom in my palm—cylindrical and light, shorter than my pinky; it looked more yellow than green up close, and bees worked all around me, pollinating the flowers that would soon become pods full of seeds. Finally, I entered the dark café, already busy, where the waitresses looked like fresh-eyed college kids and the tables featured cartoonish maps of the park. I ordered coffee and sipped from the heavy ceramic mug, rearranged my notebook and my voice recorder, and looked up too often toward the entrance.

At 8:00 sharp she walked in, easily recognizable from photos from the negotiations a dozen years earlier. She stood straight, her shoulders sloped, body wide, and she carried a thick sheaf of papers under one arm. Her cheekbones rode high and she smiled an easy smile, more sly than shy, the corners of her top lip arcing down to meet her upturned bottom one as though trying to contain the humor of it all. I stood to shake her hand and felt warmth immediately. Dishes and silverware clattered in the kitchen as we ordered breakfast and made small talk about the mesquite. She hoped for a good harvest, since the year before she'd gathered a bunch and went to borrow a mortar from Pauline to grind the beans to paste, but Pauline had lent it to someone else, and by the time she got it back and Barbara went to get her pods, they were gone.

"Gone?"

"Yeah, the pack rats got them."

We laughed. We have pack rats at home, I said. Half our supply of lentils ends up under the woodshed with miscellaneous bolts and buckles and foil pieces and, yes, thick layers of droppings. I wondered aloud if, as far as harvesting went, the Homeland Act changed things—she'd brought a copy of the entire document that sat now on the table between us, atop the cartoon map—since it specifically allowed tending and harvesting in the Furnace Creek mesquite grove and the Wildrose Canyon pinyon pine grove up higher in the mountains as well.

"Not really," she said, shrugging, sly-smiling. "We never gave up our rights to gather or whatever. We did it, and then you know they gave us trouble, but we stood our ground. We didn't back down. It's our duty to be out there on the land one-on-one."

That struck me. So often what's reclaimed has never really been lost, not totally, sometimes not at all.

She'd brought along a copy of the newsprint visitor guide that the National Park Service passes out with the fold-up map at the entrance. I had not received one. Under "Park Partners" a blurb described the ways the Timbisha tended the "beautiful but austere" landscape, how they used fire, how they cultivated "native domesticated plants"—a brand-new phrase—and cleaned springs. A small photo showed Barbara and Pauline wearing reflective vests and walking the roadside. Pauline carried a long branch, her tool for the day for clearing ditches and culverts.

"Have you talked to Pauline?" Barbara asked. "Do you have a plan to talk to Pauline?"

"Not yet."

I didn't tell her that it'd taken me a hard year to manage to arrange to speak even to her, a woman around my age with an email address and a Facebook page, a woman with an official job title with the tribe. I hadn't tried to meet Pauline Esteves because she'd be harder to reach, yes, but also because, well, here was a woman internationally known and universally respected, a woman distinguished law professor Charles Wilkinson called one of the most sophisticated human beings he'd ever met, a woman so feisty that after she led the fight to pass the Homeland Act her own tribe had voted her off the tribal council. I was, frankly, intimidated.

"Joe Kennedy invited me to his council meeting. I don't know where he's going to hold it," I said.

"He says it's in Indian Village at 11:00. That's what he said."

"Are you going?" I asked.

"I don't know," she said.

She returned to the mesquite, describing how the Timbisha followed the harvest from desert to mountains, grinding the beans into paste to make it easier to pack, and she picked up the refrain I'd heard in the visitor center movie, how this place has always been their home, even when they summered in the mountains. Recently she'd attended an evening program, she said, where a ranger gave the impression that the Timbisha didn't live in the park full-time.

"Seems like a lot of people think that," I said.

"I *know*," she said.

Barbara spoke in a familiar youthful cadence, slightly Hispanic, very Californian. "I *know*," she said, with the emphasis on *know*, a hint of uplift, part camaraderie, part incredulity, as if to imply: Can you believe it? I told her about the waitress at Denny's the previous spring who claimed there were all kinds of Indians moving around, including the ones who tossed "Indian bullets" at her, and how John the Mechanic insisted that no one could stay down in that sweltering valley in the summer.

"I *know*," she said again.

But the thing is: Barbara Durham *does* know. She grew up in Furnace Creek in Park Service housing because her father worked for the concessionaire and when they'd go see her grandmother's sister who stayed in Indian Village, this woman would have a big blanket with water running on it.

"And you could sit in back of it to be nice and cool."

She retold the history, how her people originally lived on the hillside about a mile away, near the spring but not right next to it, since that would be for the animals. But then developers wanted to build the Furnace Creek Inn, and they wanted to build it right there, of course, at the spring. You could see it from the parking lot, a much grander and more elegant place than the string of tourist shops where the café sat. The developers forced the Indians to move down the creek, where they stayed until the Park Service decided to build a visitor center—the original one in the same place as the newly renovated one—and the Indians were forced to move again.

"They told everybody they had to leave, and those who didn't get out of the way, they just went in there with a bulldozer and dug a big hole and pushed everything in."

Barbara Durham knows these stories because she's heard them retold by her elders and she knows them, too, as history. After she finished high school in Shoshone Village, fifty miles south, the school superintendent talked her into applying to Brigham Young University. She got in, but she didn't last a year. Later she headed north to attend Shasta Junior College, but eventually she came home. Soon thereafter, in the face of the looming California Desert Protection Act, the Timbisha began the long fight for recognition, and Barbara Durham joined in.

We came at last to the Homeland Act negotiations. What went wrong that first round? I asked. Why was it so difficult?

"Personalities," she said.

She described one particularly despicable character from the San Francisco office.

"What was his name?" I asked.

"I don't remember. Pauline would know. Are you going to talk to Pauline?"

"I'd like to," I said.

She moved the conversation to the second round of negotiations, the successful round. For the better part of a year, I'd been awaiting this conversation, expecting that she would see the situation differently than John Reynolds or Dick Martin did. Hers was the outsider perspective, after all, the perspective with no stake in protecting the image of government negotiators or of government in general. She'd call bullshit on their version if necessary, I was sure of it. But she didn't. Barbara Durham said almost exactly what they did: once each side honed down the team to a few essential people, everything was better. Much better. There was mutual respect, Barbara Durham said, especially with Charles Wilkinson.

"Wasn't there still anger?" I asked.

"Well, yeah. Once you work for the Park Service, you're in that mode: protect the land, protect the land. He just told them what they needed to hear."

She retold the story of when the swamp cooler broke down, the time that Dick Martin and Pauline Esteves bonded in their own way, but she also told another angle to the story.

"Those guys are out there working on it, and a big sandstorm was going on outside and Charles just had enough, and next thing you know we're looking out the window, all of us thinking: Where is he? We look out and there he is. He's just going down the road shaking his hands up in the air and talking to himself."

She laughed.

"Why?"

"He'd had it. He'd just had it. It wasn't easy, you know. But after a while, we made friends. You know, not real buddy-buddy friends, but we respected each other."

I asked if the relationship with the Park Service had improved any since the Homeland Act passed, and she said that it had, but there are always so many new employees moving in and others moving away—land-based agencies, ironically enough, don't value rootedness much—that many Park Service people, even at the highest levels, don't know about the Homeland Act or the Timbisha or how to include them.

"I saw you in the movie over at the new visitor center."

"I *know*."

"Are you happy about how that came out?"

"Yeah. We're working on the exhibits. We've got some pictures from when we were doing the protests."

"I noticed how they kind of gloss over the struggle some."

"I *know*. They gloss over today. They talk about yesterday."

By "yesterday" she meant hundreds or thousands of years ago. And I could see her point. Aside from the movie, the visitor center still had little information about the Timbisha today and none whatsoever about the thirty-year battle to reclaim their homeland. The generous explanation would be that the Park Service hasn't figured out how to acknowledge that history, how to frame it. Barbara Durham's point about the park's interpretive staff—the rangers who give talks and walks and create displays—changing so often is probably crucial. If no one knows the history, how can they shape it for public consumption? The more realistic explanation might be that the Park Service, and maybe the general public, the millions of visitors who love Death Valley with a passion, aren't ready to move away from the focus on the dramatic scenery and the feel-good pioneer tales: the twenty-mule trains, crazy Scotty and his so-called castle. Either way, the Timbisha themselves are one obvious source for setting the record straight, and Barbara Durham in particular would be invaluable. She's studied history and lived it, too.

"We want to be involved," she said. "But how can we now that I'm no longer THPO?" Tribal historic preservation officer. She pronounced the acronym "tippo."

I was confused. "I thought that was your job."

"It was, but they took it away."

By "they" she meant the new tribal council. It seemed impossibly frustrating, infuriating even, that after all those years of battling the Park Service, Barbara Durham would have to watch her good work—and her very livelihood—get stymied by internal squabbling. "Some people call it 'Indian politics,'" Charles Wilkinson told me when I asked him about the lack of progress in the years after the Homeland Act. "But it's just politics." Change takes time, he implied. Be patient and not judgmental. That made sense from a distance, but up close like this, the situation seemed dire, dire personally for Barbara Durham, dire for the other Timbisha living in Furnace Creek, and dire for the entire enterprise.

"I think they're scared of me," Barbara said.

Tribal leaders had good reason to be scared of Barbara Durham. Here sat a woman who'd personally persuaded a U.S. senator to add an amendment to an act of Congress. She'd sat on boards and attended negotiations. Now she was helping create visitor center displays for no pay, and once her unemployment runs out, she said, she could end up waiting tables right here in the café.

I looked around. Every table in the place was occupied on a Tuesday morning. There were athletic types in bike shorts, families with babies in high chairs, a group of city-dressed young adults speaking loudly in a foreign language. One man dining alone asked his young waitress to pose for a selfie with him. She set down a large armful of dishes to smile wide, face to face with a stranger.

"Busy place," I said.

"I *know*. It never stops these days. Used to be summer was downtime. Not anymore. Now the international tourists come year-round."

"Don't you ever get tired of it?"

"No," she said with a shrug. "I kind of like it."

Home is home, she seemed to say, not some idealized past, not some preserved wilderness, not even tended wilderness, but this place, right here, where the two-dollar tip hits the cartoon map. Alive, not dead. Barbara Durham, in her matter-of-factness, seemed to embody the way reclaiming requires the ability to shift perspective over time, to persist beyond triumph even with mixed results or downright lousy ones.

"Well, let's go see Pauline. You can follow me." She stood and fished for her keys, and I tried to hide my anxiety as I followed her, walking at a fast clip toward her pickup truck. I had not expected to meet Pauline today. I had not planned for it. Barbara Durham must've noticed my uncertainty. She slowed as we crossed the fast-filling parking area and said that Pauline should be at home, that she's still very active, cutting firewood with an axe. Just a regular person, she seemed to suggest.

"But sometimes she says things you don't understand."

"Like a philosopher?" I asked.

She hopped onto the running board, swung herself into the cab, and gestured for me to follow her.

"Yeah, I guess," she said. "Me, I just like plain talk."

Pauline Esteves sat beneath a broad swath of cloud-streaked sky at a small round table outside a single-wide trailer wearing a red housedress. Her walker sat beside her.

"This is the writer I told you about," Barbara said.

Pauline looked up, her eyes intelligent and distrustful, her thin white hair combed straight and clipped to one side. Her skin, which in photos looked lined, stretched smooth across high wide cheekbones the rich hue of sun-darkened pine. She did not smile. She did not respond.

"So I'm gonna go. I'll see you later," Barbara said, giving me a kind look, somewhere between pity and amusement.

Then we were alone, Pauline Esteves and me. The birds made a racket. The wind blew. Behind her stood a pile of firewood of various lengths with some skinny limbs newly cut. Before her sat a notepad, a ballpoint pen, and a stack of photos she'd been labeling. She stood and crumpled some newspaper to crush a trail of red ants and wipe them from around her photos and off the table. They were small and fast and when I asked if they bite she said that they do.

"They definitely do," she repeated.

Silence.

She sat and picked up her pen, and stared hard through her light-sensitive glasses at the photo in front of her.

"I spent the night at Texas Spring," I said.

"Hmm," she said. "I used to go up there to check the mesquites because they're *protected*." She emphasized the last word with such force that I wasn't sure what she'd said. Her voice was deep and gruff with a hint of an accent, Spanish, maybe, or her native tongue.

"Protected?"

She nodded. I thought she meant by legislation.

"Like preserved?"

She shook her head disgustedly.

"From the *wind*." Like an obscenity.

More silence.

"I want to know about the Homeland Act and . . ."

"What I want to know," she said, dropping her ballpoint and turning her gaze hard on me, "is what's your *pos-i-tion* on all this."

I launched into my spiel, how my interest lay in reclaiming—to take back, to make right, to make useful—and what a perfect example the Homeland Act was. A triumph really.

Pauline interrupted with a soft *hrrmpf* sound which sounded like neither approval nor disapproval, more like weariness. My premise suddenly sounded shallow and naïve, and I didn't know what to do but start at the beginning.

"When did you become an activist?" I asked.

"I always was," she said. And we were off.

She told me how she was sent to a boarding school, briefly, in Stewart, Nevada, the kind of place where Native kids were stripped of language and identity and sometimes mistreated physically. Beverly Ogle wrote about those schools, but she hadn't been forced to attend. Pauline Esteves had. I wondered how she had survived so intact. Because her father came and rescued her, she said, and brought her back to Furnace Creek, and not long after she returned the family was forced to move from their home because they were too close to the highway.

"Because we were an *eyesore*."

She was eleven then. The year was 1936. She remembers one faucet in the middle of the yard in Indian Village and one community toilet.

"So in order to go use a flushing toilet I had to walk around here, way down here." She gestured out across the open space between her trailer and some tree-shaded adobe homes a few hundred feet away. "I don't know. A long way."

"So your folks were alive then?"

"Uh-huh. Yeah. And they were supposed to do the same thing. Elderly people and all that. And then they had a laundry there too and then they had to make hot water on a wood heater and then we were told not to be gathering wood."

I laughed. I couldn't help it.

She laughed, too. "It was so *ridiculous* that people joked about it."

She eased her way through the stories toward the heyday of the activism, the late 1960s and early 1970s. In 1968, Dennis Banks and other Chippewa started the American Indian Movement—AIM—to help combat hunger and alcoholism, to work on housing and education, but their activism soon turned more aggressive. AIM protesters occupied Alcatraz in 1970 and made the nightly news posing with superstar supporters like Marlon Brando and Jane Fonda. Though the occupation fizzled under pressure from drugs and infighting and the lousy San Francisco weather, it was a start. Within a year, AIM held protests at Mount Rushmore and Plymouth Rock, and Russell Means and Dennis Banks led a group of Sioux from the Pine Ridge reservation in South Dakota in the much-publicized takeover of Wounded Knee, a confrontation that ended in a seventy-one-day standoff with the FBI.

Pauline was traveling then, lobbying Indian Health Services, attending conferences, trying to join forces with other tribes in conflict with the Park Service, like the Alwahneechee in Yosemite who'd been burned out. She went to Alcatraz in the early 1970s during the protests and saw the canoes the activists used to get over to the island and back. She told the stories with enthusiasm and humor and a hint of bravado.

"We ran this little car to pieces, a real nice little Toyota, and it just fell to pieces."

After that, they hitchhiked and took buses, lived on nothing; they never stopped trying, never stopped speaking up.

Look at these stories one way, the way I've been looking at them since driving past that Homeland sign with my mother, and they're always moving toward a climax, a happy-ever-after ending. There's a heroic subtext, and to meet Pauline Esteves is to know you're in the presence of someone who matters, someone who made a difference. I couldn't wait to hear how she would describe the negotiations.

She started by recalling the notorious meeting on the buckets in the fire cache.

"To this day I don't know what they were thinking. It was *ridiculous*." She shook her head and again smiled ruefully.

I urged her on. After that, the tribe brought in the big guns, right? I said. They made things happen? There was one famous protest in 1996 when the Timbisha Shoshone and supporters marched down Highway 190 in hundred-degree weather passing out leaflets, carrying signs saying "This Is Our Homeland" and "Cultural Respect Not Cultural Genocide." What about that? She evaded the questions. What about the second negotiations? I asked. I tried to get her to linger, to talk about Reynolds or Wilkinson, but she kept digressing, giving short answers, nudging the conversation away. I wasn't going to get details, and I didn't need them. I knew that story by heart. And she knew it; she could tell I did. Still, I prompted her for a feel-good quote.

"And now the land is yours," I said.

"And what have we done since the year of 2000?" she asked.

I didn't know how to reply.

"Nothing. We've done nothing."

"That's a tragic story," I said.

"Nobody knows."

"Nobody knows the story?"

"Nobody knows the reason why."

"What do you think the reason is?"

"Because of this group of people and their greed."

In an attempt to balance out the huge discrepancy in wealth between California tribes that have casinos and those that don't, California gaming tribes decided to form a pot of money for non-gaming tribes, money that's intended for economic development. The Timbisha received some of the money, but Pauline did not approve of how it was being distributed.

"Economic development, my foot! They just want the money."

Pauline grew more intense, less animated. She stopped saying "ridiculous" altogether.

"But there's Joe's council," I said. "He invited me to the meeting. Are you going to go?"

"I don't know." She sighed heavily and balled her hands in her lap. For the first time, she looked tired.

Back when she was on the council, she said, they had plans to build a tourist lodge, a kind of base camp for environmental learning groups. They wanted to create jobs and to educate people about their history, but the others, they weren't interested. They wanted monthly checks. Period.

"That gaming money has just made people just go crazy. All the small California tribes, they've become divided just like we are. Sometimes the way we feel is we should just pull out, disenroll ourselves."

This constituted a bit of backwards reasoning, or perhaps underscored Pauline's contrary nature, since "disenrolling" has become an ugly and disturbingly regular phenomenon among gaming tribes trying to keep tribal rolls small and thereby keep their own checks big. They comb through the lists looking for names to scratch off for not having enough Native blood or the right paperwork, any reason at all. I'd never heard of a person or a group of people wanting to disenroll themselves.

"What would you have then?" I asked.

"Nothing."

I'd known things were bad, but I'd come with my own agenda, ignoring that fact. I thought of my odd revelation in the night, about not coming into a place with expectations; it had taken Pauline Esteves two hours to make me understand.

"This is the present," she said. "I was taught: Don't always be talking about the past. Sure, it's a good foundation, but go forward. You talk about the circle of life. See, we're not going through that circle at all. We're not moving. We're stuck."

She paused.

"We were told in one of the legends that we were going to be stuck sometimes," she said at last, "but never to give up. If you fall, get up, and if there's something in your way go around it, and that's what we're trying to do."

A distant engine rumbled close and dust blew high into the air, obscuring the Panamints, as a single car drove off the pavement and onto the gravel across the Village.

"There's Joe in his mountain car. I love that old car. We used to do a lot of hunting in that car. So he's heading down toward Grace's. I hear the dogs barking. You better go."

"You're not coming?"

She turned her attention back to the stack of photos she'd been labeling for the visitor center display, holding them with one hand to keep them from blowing away, pressing hard on the ballpoint with the other.

"I got work to do," she said.

10

What Now?

Death Valley, California—March 2012

J oe Kennedy's mountain car, a boxy black Chevy Suburban sun-baked gray, looked to be the hardest-worked vehicle in Indian Village. I trailed it, and the sound of barking dogs, around a short dirt bend from Pauline's trailer to where Joe Kennedy now sat beside Grace Goad at a round table under a porch awning, with an empty chair and a cell phone flipped open between them. Grace introduced herself, half-stood beside her walker—another elder, another walker—to shake my hand, and invited me to sit in the empty chair.

Grace Goad's name was as familiar to me as Barbara's or Pauline's since, like them, she participated in the Homeland negotiations from beginning to end. She'd served on several tribal councils since that time, been voted on, been voted off. She should look world-weary, I thought, or cynical. Instead she looked steady and observant as we sat together in front of her adobe home.

A large tree shaded the yard, a deep-grooved red trunk with long thick limbs that dipped groundward and reached outward. Beneath it the dogs lolled in sand, finished with their barking like their work for the day.

"Nice tree," I said.

A beat of silence followed before Joe Kennedy finally spoke. He explained that the tree was a salt cedar, non-native, that nothing could grow beneath it. Salt cedars suck up the water table and outcompete the native cottonwoods and willows, he said.

"But I can't cut it down," Grace said. "It's the only shade I've got."

Joe Kennedy did not argue. Tall and round-shouldered with a goatee, a long black ponytail, and a handsome chin-jutted smile, he seemed the kind of man women might call a teddy bear to soften his size, but while that description might fit his easy bearing—he leaned back in his chair and cupped his hands in his lap rather than crossing his arms across his chest—his manner belied diminution. There was urgency about him, not anger so much as an eagerness to speak the truth. About salt cedars. About Indian history. About everything. He did not suffer fools, and he did not hesitate to confront misinformation, but he also did not argue with his elders, so he held his tongue about Grace Goad's tree.

A few teenagers loitered in the house, but did not come out; television noise roiled as background. A middle-aged woman, Grace's daughter perhaps, emerged and unfolded a low aluminum beach chair near the dogs. She faced away from us, cradled a small notebook in her lap, and did not speak.

Joe Kennedy began a slow preface. No calling to order. No taking minutes. Unless that's what the beach chair woman was up to. He'd heard about my project, and this meeting seemed mostly for my benefit.

"As far as reclaiming, we'd have to say 'recognized' because we don't have all of our lands that the Timbisha occupied years ago."

A third member of the renegade council, Erick Mason, chimed in on speaker phone. He couldn't miss work—he works for Cal Trans, the state department of transportation—and as the conversation went on, he monitored a scanner in the background. He was hard to hear, but as I'd soon learn, he possessed an unfailing knack for candor and concision.

"The word 'reclaiming' glorifies the situation, makes it seem like we got everything that we wanted. That isn't the case," he said.

His reproach struck the same chord as Pauline's gruff, resigned *hmmrff*. I looked over at Grace, who kept her gaze fixed on the horizon.

"You should look up the original number, what we were after," he said.

Reclaimers

I knew what number he meant: 160,000. That's the acreage the tribe requested in a 1993 proposal to Congress. The number was up, way up, from the 2,000 acres they'd requested a few short years earlier, and this request came on the heels of one in which the Park Service had deigned to consider only 60 acres. The move reflected the tribe's exasperation and desire to be taken seriously as well as the genuine belief that, really, 160,000 acres is a whole lot less land than their ancestors had inhabited since time eternal. The move also reflected a larger movement. Around the same time, the Western Shoshone National Council, to which the Timbisha belong, submitted documents to the courts showing that the Treaty of Ruby Valley of 1863 had granted the Shoshone title to a huge chunk of the West stretching from southern California to southern Idaho and that the Shoshone had never ceded that title.

"So how did Europeans in Death Valley get ahold of the land in the first place?" I asked.

"It was a lot of theft. You might as well say theft," Joe Kennedy said. "Either murder, theft, intimidation, anything they could use to push the people off of those lands."

He launched into a story to illustrate his point.

"I had an archaeologist tell me how they found a can with a note in it, how this one guy had murdered a whole family of fifteen Shoshones to get their springs, and in this note he had written how he had tricked these Shoshones and put arsenic in their sugar and murdered them all and now he owned the spring. So those kinds of things happened, but it's not documented, it's not reported."

"Like this spring up here," Grace added. "The old people used to live up there a long time ago."

She gestured across the valley floor to where we could see Furnace Creek Inn, the yellow stucco buildings, the red Spanish-tiled rooflines, and the green fringe of palms. You could imagine the blue swimming pool, too, aligned horizontally to mirror the sharp lines of the backdrop where ridge meets sky.

"Where the Inn is?" I asked.

"Above the Inn. Way above the Inn. About probably half a mile, or was that a mile? I can't tell. The spring used to run down through there, and that was the old people's spring, and they took it away from them. What were they called?"

I didn't know what word she was fishing for: bastards, thieves, whites, Europeans, miners, assholes? Grace addressed the woman in the beach chair, "You know who I mean."

"Forty-niners," the woman said without turning around.

"That's it, the forty-niners," Grace said.

Then she launched into a story of her own.

"All the Indians ran from the spring. They were camping up there when the forty-niners came in, and they had to leave fast, and they left a little old lady up there. So they came in, the forty-niners, and they treated her good."

"They did?" I asked.

"Yeah," Grace Goad said.

"My dad told me that story," Joe said. "He said the soldiers weren't there to keep the peace. They were there to rape the women. So everybody left camp, and the old lady stayed to keep the fire burning, and when they came back, they found the soldiers had mutilated that little old lady."

"I never heard about soldiers," Grace said. "I heard that she was blind and they had to leave her there because she was blind."

"She couldn't keep up," Joe said.

"So they treated her good," Grace said. "That was the forty-niners."

The two versions of the story captured the central tension in Death Valley. There are the good stories and the not-good stories. People want to believe the early white settlers were heroic survivors who meant no harm or at worst goofy eccentrics like Death Valley Scotty. The stories you rarely hear are the truly heinous ones: rape, murder, plunder. The good stories and the bad stories never quite square up in the West, and they weren't squaring up in the salt cedar–shaded space between the generations either.

Cooperate or fight? There's no easy answer. Grace Goad had lived her entire life under the heavy hand of the Park Service. Despite the oppression, she'd learned to respect the likes of Dick Martin or John Reynolds and to cooperate with them. If she hadn't, there'd be no Homeland Act. Joe Kennedy's grandfather helped build Scotty's Castle; his great-grandfather lived on land that would become the Nevada Test Site, where 928 underground tests of nuclear weapons took place in the second half of the twentieth century. As a result Joe Kennedy had fought for and won affected status for his tribe at Yucca Mountain, a move that helped prevent long-term storage of nuclear waste on the sacred site. If he hadn't, his people might be drinking irradiated water or worse.

"There was another story," Joe Kennedy continued. "I guess the forty-niners got over here somehow and when they were leaving they didn't have any food or water. The Indians tried to give them water, but got shot at by those forty-niners and so they said heck with them and left them. They didn't try to help any more. I guess that's how this place came to be called Death Valley," he said.

"But they didn't have to die here," I said.

"Right," said Grace Goad, and she laughed a little.

"Right," said Joe Kennedy. He did not laugh.

"Are you still there, Erick?" I asked.

"Yeah, I figured you probably didn't want to hear my other traffic."

"What other traffic?" Joe asked.

Erick's voice changed tone, dropped into a conspiratorial sing-song the way a native Bostonian or Texan slips into an accent when passing on local gossip, as he recounted what he was hearing on the scanner, how the cops had come onto the Bishop reservation to harass some kids for underage drinking.

"Oh my god," said Grace.

"Yeah, they're straight out of the academy in Southern California, these young cops." Erick said.

"Isn't there a jurisdiction issue there?" I asked.

"They're under PL 280."

Public Law 280 gives certain states, including California, police jurisdiction on Indian land. What might seem a small matter to outsiders—who cares who cracks down on kids' drinking as long as someone does?—is a huge matter to Native Americans. The law passed in 1953 in tandem with other termination laws, and its intention was clear. In *Blood Struggle* Charles Wilkinson describes the passage of PL 280 and the reaction to it matter of factly: "Tribal leaders saw it for what it was: a direct attack on tribal sovereignty." Tribes have struggled for decades to get out from under PL 280. One of the biggest arguments is that non-Indian police don't address domestic violence on the reservations.

"What is it? One in three Indian women will be abused or raped in their lifetime," Joe Kennedy said. "And it's not by their people. It's by outsiders. People run to reservations because they can get away with things they couldn't get away with somewhere else."

Research, I'd later learn, backed him up: one in three.

Grace leaned forward trying to overhear Erick's scanner through the cell phone as Joe continued to direct the conversation toward me, touting his council and the good it could do.

"That's one of the things we were working on. We had a couple of meetings with Park Service, the Inyo County sheriff's department, CHP, BLM, Nevada highway patrol, FBI."

"Whatever happened to that?"

"We ran into all this trouble with gaming. Well. . . ." He paused. "It just really put a division with the people. Gaming could've been a really good thing if it was done properly and we didn't have these outside agitators that came in . . ."

He ran one hand over his head and slumped in his chair like a boxer after a tough round, and then he launched into the troubles. The casino deal? The one proposed in 2002? Well, he said, the developer didn't show up out of nowhere. He was *brought in*—Joe emphasized this phrase the way Pauline said "ridiculous" and Barbara said "I know"—by a former BIA official who would receive a cut of the profits if the deal went through. And the second casino? The one proposed in 2007? No better. Threats and defamation, bribery, and, on the periphery, even a murder. Government officials at the highest levels were involved. Blame shifted from the BIA to the DOI, the Department of the Interior, the department that oversees both the BIA and the NPS. An escalation of acronyms.

My head ached the way it used to in algebra class, where you're good for a few pages of problems as long as they follow the same pattern, but at some point integers collide with variables and coefficients and constants. Solve for X. It sounds easy. But it kept getting more difficult. Part of the problem was my own exhaustion; it was my third interview of the day. I was hungry and tired. But there was something more at work. I wanted to figure out what it was.

Joe Kennedy continued his story. Sometime between the first and second casino proposals, new names began to appear on the tribal rolls mysteriously, people who did not, according to this tribal council, meet the criteria for tribal membership laid out in the new constitution.

"We looked at the names and we were like, 'Hey, those guys aren't Timbisha.'"

"How did they get on the tribal rolls?" I asked.

"We don't know," Joe said.

"There's no way to go back and say here's what the constitution says?"

"Yeah, that has happened. . . ."

He and Erick competed to give the play-by-play, which council said what to whom in what year, and I couldn't help but think it had begun to feel like a family squabble, the kind of skirmish where there's no way to know who's in the right. I could not scribble dates or names fast enough, so I set down my pen.

"So what's the total enrollment now?"

At that point, the Death Valley faction counted 265 valid members; the official council claimed 380. To Joe Kennedy, that amounts to over a hundred questionable members, including George Gholson, the current tribal chairperson.

"But he believes himself to be a member. And he's someone you've known your whole lives."

"No," Joe said.

"No, no," Grace said. She was emphatic on the point. "We never knew him."

"He's a stranger," Joe said. "He just popped into the picture."

"What's his interest?"

"Gaming. Gaming. This all happened right when the former Department of Interior guy brought in the casino developers. That's what caused all this mess."

This seemed a far step above tribal infighting. Joe Kennedy was suggesting an out-and-out conspiracy.

"Why would the Department of Interior cause all this trouble?"

"Because gaming is not the whole story. You've heard of the Western Shoshone Claims Distribution Act of 2004?"

I had. The act entitled the tribe to money in exchange for land, water, and mineral rights encroached upon over a century. A group led by Kennedy refused to accept payment—How could money make up for what had been lost? Wasn't it yet another lousy treaty?—and sued. But just a month earlier, while I was comfortably ensconced in Marin County, a federal judge determined that the so-called Kennedy faction had no legal standing.

Now I was beginning to get it: Joe Kennedy believed government officials helped put a tribal council in place that would accept the payments and put the issue to rest. I had to admit his theory sounded perfectly plausible. Proving it would be difficult, maybe impossible. But was the theory plausible? Definitely.

Still, there was the math to deal with. Whether there were 265 members or 380, it sounded like there were still plenty of undisputed tribal members voting for Gholson. I tried to bring this up, who the people are, what they might want.

"One thing you have to understand about our people," Erick said, "is they're very, very poor; there aren't too many middle-class people amongst us. It's a struggle. In the last census only 10 or 12 percent of us claimed to have full-time work. Housing is a big issue."

In the preface to the *Draft Secretarial Report to Congress*, April 1999, Pauline Esteves wrote: "Most important of all, I envision that this plan will bring the people closer together. Many of us will be able to live and work in tribal communities once again."

By all outward appearances, the Homeland Act had done precisely the opposite.

Reclaimers

The heat began to rise and flat light washed the scenery. As noon approached, grandchildren appeared and served us bologna sandwiches with potato chips, and cold water in plastic cups. Erick Mason spoke his mind over the phone in the table center while we chewed and swallowed and tried not to crunch chips too loudly, and as he did, the conversation grew broader in scope.

"They're making it so we can't live the old ways," Erick said.

"They" was no longer just the new tribal council but oppressors, from big government to big corporations; the dangers ranged from mining contamination to seed sterilization.

"One thing, the recession hasn't been such a bad thing for Indians because we're already at poverty level, but what they're taking away from us is our ability to survive even at the poverty level," Erick said.

"Right," Grace said.

"I think that's what happens when you don't listen to your elders, you don't know who your people are, where you're from, how did you survive, what is your history, what is your folklore, mythology. All of that. When you don't have that, you don't see. You're like sheep. You can be taken advantage of."

I looked around for the grandchildren, wondering how this talk sounded from their vantage point, but the kids had long since retreated inside.

I turned to face Grace Goad.

"What do you want? " I asked. "What now?"

"I want it all back," she said. She held her small fist in the air and pounded it gently against the air, the cedar tree swaying behind and above her. "We want it back."

Later I'd look up the salt cedar, a tree I thought I had never heard of, and realize it was a tamarisk, the most familiar invasive species in the Southwest, one that lines nearly every creek bed and covers more than 900,000 acres, one brought in from the Middle East as an ornamental and later used for erosion control that then spread willy-nilly and took over everywhere. But I'd only ever known it as a bush, never a tree as big as an oak. The parallel was obvious: greed on the individual scale is one thing, on the institutional level it can grow so large it's impossible to see that it's poisonous. Unless you're living right underneath it. Where nothing can grow.

III

When the Walls Come
Tumbling Down

11

Unequivocal

Vancouver, Washington—March 2012

Drive through Oregon south to north and what you notice most, besides the rain, is rivers. Starting in the far north of California, I-5 crosses over them and runs beside them. Klamath, Rogue, Umpqua, Willamette, McKenzie, Columbia. As a college student newly arrived from the desert, the rivers astounded me. I stood by the Willamette, brimming full, surface swirling, and gawked. For the four years I lived in Oregon for college, I jogged and biked by the Willamette daily, and I never stopped being awed by the sheer volume of moving water in the state, so alive, so enticing, so seemingly wild.

But those rivers aren't wild. Not the way river advocates define a wild river, as "relatively untouched by development." They're all dammed. At least for now. There are four wildly controversial dams on the main stem of the Klamath. Three smaller dams have been removed from the Rogue—four if you include the one dynamited by saboteurs in 1912—and one remains. Eight dams remain on the North Umpqua, including Soda Springs: cracked, patched, and recommended for removal by the Forest Service, but still standing. Six line the McKenzie. And the Willamette? The most visible of Oregon's rivers, the one that flows north through the fertile namesake valley teeming with two-thirds of the state's population and smack through the middle of Portland to dump into the Columbia

River, has a whopping thirteen federal dams. I somehow missed this fact even when I visited the river every single day.

Which puts me in the same camp, I'd suspect, as most Americans. Back home in Washington's North Cascades, I'd taught writing seminars at an environmental learning center on the shores of Diablo Lake, within sight of an enormous hydroelectric dam, where students described the reservoir water, the milky turquoise of glacial silt, and the former creeks that pour down road cuts like waterfalls. They described the wildlife, the trees, the wind, the sky, the clouds, but never the power lines—humongous this close to the source and buzzing loudly overhead—upon which their regular lives depend.

I was as guilty as anyone. The three dams that line the Skagit—Gorge, Diablo, and Ross—are all more or less visible from the North Cascades Highway, a road I'd driven a thousand times over the years. I'd once lived along the highway, and I used to work for the national park that straddles the highway, and for one interminable summer when Laurie worked on the east side of the crest and I worked on the west, I commuted over the highway. But I'd mostly ignored the dams. So when I saw that a class would be offered on their history I signed right up. My image of dam builders before the class was that they were creatures of their times, wed to conventional, and ultimately wrong-minded, ideas about progress. Then I learned about J. D. Ross.

J. D. Ross hailed from tiny Chatham, Ontario, where he'd been a precocious kid fascinated by electricity, playing Ben Franklin with kites and strings, designing his first battery at eleven and testing it on house cats, a story that was the worst ever told of him during a long public life. The son of a nurseryman, he graduated college at nineteen and headed to the Klondike for a fling with adventure before landing in Seattle. There, in 1908, with no experience whatsoever, he presented himself to the city's young power company as an engineer. Within three years, he was superintendent of Seattle City Light.

By 1912, Seattle had maxed out the power potential of all the close rivers, but advances were afoot. Tesla's new three-phase AC current allowed engineers to increase voltage in transmission lines, reduce the line current and size of conductors, and, as a result, carry power a much longer distance. Like from the Skagit to Seattle. The only issues were who would fund such projects, who would build them, and who would profit.

Early power plants in Washington State were privately owned. They'd been constructed to power interurban railroads, and as the railroads connected, the power companies merged to form Puget Sound Power and Light, which was purchased by a Boston investment firm, Stone & Webster. All of which was fine and good. Except that the electricity was expensive, the quality poor. The *Seattle Times* complained bitterly: "Seattle is a miserably lighted town."

When J. D. Ross headed up the Skagit in 1912, he could see the potential right away: the narrow gorge, the steep drop. Access might be difficult, but a railroad could be punched in. The only real problem was getting permits since Stone & Webster held them all.

J. D. Ross had technical chops. He had the foresight to plan for not one, but three dams total on the river—one for storage and two more to regulate flow—and he thought to fit the dams with needle valves halfway up to release siltation, long before anyone was worried about silt. But he had political prowess, too. He leaped headlong into trying to convince the powers that be that the permits would be better off in the hands of the public. The city was glad to support him. A *Seattle Times* editorial heralded city ownership as a defense against the attack waged by "the Boston Syndicate" plunderers. Eventually Ross triumphed over Stone & Webster. Calvin Coolidge started the generators running at Gorge Dam from the White House with a golden key in 1924, Diablo Dam followed in 1936, and within twenty years, Seattle had more available electricity at less cost than any other major metropolitan area in the country.

J. D. Ross put power, literally, in the hands of the people.

I'd intended to head straight from Death Valley to Vancouver, Washington, an ambitious plan but not an impossible one, until a belt began to squeak under the hood of the Buick. Actually, it'd been squeaking for over three hundred miles, squawking more like it, caterwauling. I raced along

I-80, the belt squealing like an injured animal, cruising at eighty miles per hour, when suddenly the squeak stopped cold. A loud bash sounded under the hood—was this déjà vu?—and I watched in the rearview mirror as a metal object bounced and rolled off into the center barricade. I coasted to the slow lane, took an off-ramp, and found a Pep Boys open on Saturday. A lanky redheaded boy in coveralls showed me where the water pump pulley had broken loose.

"Whoever did this should pay," he said.

I pictured John the Mechanic back in Beatty. He'd replaced the water pump the day before, and I'd even called him from the road when the squeak began. What should I do? I asked. Don't worry about it, he slurred.

"Everyone knows to use Loctite," said the redhead. "You know what Loctite is?"

"I do," I said.

I made it only as far as Medford, Oregon, then in the morning continued on my way, racing north through Oregon, past all those rivers, and finally to Vancouver, where Laurie was working on yet another small-scale apple tree reclamation project.

The Old Apple Tree is called just that (OAT in the government email chains) and is a beloved fixture in Vancouver. The tree was planted in 1826 from seeds collected at dessert by a dinner guest at Fort Vancouver, a bustling Hudson's Bay Company trade center, and is thought to be the oldest apple tree in a region known for its apple industry. Its trunk is as wide around as a culvert and, since suffering severe storm damage a few years back, the tree lists hard to the west; its tallest branch reaches no more than fifteen feet from the ground. It sits below a railroad grade over which trains clatter regularly, and a freeway jammed with traffic all hours of the day, and under the final approach to Portland International Airport. It sits within sight of the I-5 bridge over the Columbia in the middle of a concrete courtyard—the Old Apple Tree Park—surrounded by a heavy low-hanging chain, decorative and fittingly historic, but since the chain was doing no good, there's now a chain-link fence around that.

It's a sad sight, and it's hard not to feel sorry for the tree, to wish for a way to set it free like a river or a zoo animal, but there's something charming about the pride Vancouver takes in it. Each year the city hosts an Old Apple Tree Festival complete with a community cider pressing. Two years in a row, the local paper, the *Columbian*, ran a front-page story about Laurie's "expert" repair work on the tree.

Laurie hates being called an expert. She works for the Park Service and the tree is managed by the Park Service, which brought her down to try to help. At home, in the historic orchard she manages, she'd been helping old trees maintain their structure by grafting scion wood into the bark on one side of a wound and then into bark somewhere above the wound to allow nutrients to flow through the cambium. She's done hundreds of such grafts, some of them artistically crisscrossed, most of them successful. But the ones on the Old Apple Tree were more difficult because of the toughness of the tree bark and also because of the audience. Park Service officials, reporters, and local contractors who prune the tree each spring watched while she worked. No one expressed cynicism in person, but the weekly arts magazine featured an essay written from the tree's point of view protesting the rough treatment. Poked and prodded. Chained in. Surrounded by cement. In the end, none of it mattered since vandals yanked the grafts out. That's the reason for the chainlink fence. That's also the reason Laurie was back for a second time.

The next day, while Laurie worked, I sat in the Vancouver Public Library scrolling through articles about the Condit dam removal from the White Salmon River. The White Salmon bisects the bottom hem of Washington State about sixty miles east of Vancouver. It's a short river, only forty-six miles from the headwaters on the glacier flanks of Mount Adams to where it empties into the Columbia River directly across from Hood River, Oregon. Yakama Indian historians claim it was once home to eight thousand salmon and steelhead each year, but by the 1970s the fish hadn't come upriver for decades. Not since 1912 when Condit dam, the lone dam on the river, was built.

In 1976, Klickitat Public Utility District submitted a proposal for six more dams on the river. To the engineers and public officials, the proposal must've seemed like nothing out of the ordinary. By the 1970s, hundreds of dams had been built along the Columbia and its tributaries, making the Pacific Northwest the hydropower capital of the world. This, by comparison, was small beans. But to some people, the proposal was not ordinary, not small beans. Opposition rose fast, not in Portland or Seattle, those urban hotbeds of activism, but in tiny Trout Lake, home to a few hundred residents—farmers and loggers mostly—who passed their days within sight of the river. Friends of the White Salmon River formed in Trout Lake, and members handwrote letters and held living-room meetings and contacted newspapers and did not back down.

Why? Maybe the proposal's timing was wrong; the historical tide was turning. It's hard to believe from the bead-eye of history that in the bicentennial, the same year Pauline Esteves riled Death Valley tourists by tugging at their conservationist heartstrings and Jimmy Carter donned his cardigan in the White House, dam-building enthusiasts could still run on such long leashes. Six new dams on forty-six river miles? No way. Not anymore. Friends of the White Salmon River defeated the proposal and took on a larger foe, the existing dam, the fish blocker: Condit. That battle would take another thirty-five years.

Most of the articles I found in the library database appeared in the *Columbian* or the *Seattle Times*—national attention turned to Condit only during the breaching and lasted only a short while—and many focused on Phyllis Clausen. One article referred to the eighty-seven-year-old as a "conservation superhero" and another cited her as the "driving force" behind the long struggle to remove the dam. Soon I'd learn she didn't care much for the superlatives, but judging by the sheer number of times her name appeared in the newspapers, she played a major role.

I stood looking out through fogged library windows at downtown Vancouver. At one point, Condit had been the largest dam in the nation slated for removal. The fact that few people had heard of it felt somehow fitting. Outside on the street rain fell steadily, planes headed for Portland roared overhead, and a few blocks away, along the Columbia River, longshoremen loaded barges. Vancouver's downtown has been refurbished in recent years—there's a new paved trail by the river, a few upscale hotels and restaurants, even a Maya Lin–designed walkway near

Fort Vancouver—but Vancouver remains the unassuming working-class sister city to Portland across the river. Easy to overlook.

Later that afternoon, I stood inside the foyer at the clubhouse of the 55-plus community where Phyllis Clausen now lives and watched as she approached, walking across the rain-spattered parking lot, the gray-saturated world, wearing a purple raincoat and a black knit beret. She was slight and purposeful, a lifelong walker by the looks of it. She entered through the raindrop-streaked door, shook out her umbrella, and suggested a cozy place inside to sit. We could hear the sound of a raucous card game, or maybe bingo, in the large dining room glassed off from us, but it didn't bother Phyllis. She bent forward, knees together and pointed my way, and spoke in a labored voice, enunciating with raspy precision, pausing frequently. If you didn't know any better, the word "frail" might come to mind.

She began her story at the beginning.

One glorious Fourth of July weekend in the early 1970s, Phyllis Clausen got her first glimpse of the White Salmon River. If it was not love at first sight, it was something very close. She and her husband, Vic, had moved from Minnesota to Vancouver, and after a few years, they began looking for a place where they could get away from the city. At first they considered land in Oregon where they could grow filberts. They checked out the area, the fertile rolling farmland, tested the soil, even made a couple of offers, but nothing panned out. Then one day they went to go pick cherries. Someone told them there were good ones up the White Salmon.

"We'd never been there, so it was just an excursion, and after we'd picked cherries we saw this road that was leading north, and we began going up the road. And kept going and kept going and kept going."

She leaned her head back, clasped her hands together, and laughed with delight at the memory.

"It was the most gorgeous day, sunshine, and we could see Mount Adams in the distance and we kept getting drawn toward it."

They rumbled along side roads, into the forest and out, and finally along the river, which is stunning even by Northwest standards, cutting through black basalt cliffs, rugged and moss-covered, and churning over waterfalls. When at last they entered Trout Lake and found twenty acres for sale, Phyllis and Vic Clausen agreed right then and there: this was it. They bought the property and began to spend every single weekend and holiday there; they planted trees, firs and pines, five acres a year, and bought more land as it came up for sale until eventually they owned fifty-seven acres, much of it along the river. They loved the land and the people, too; they joined in potlucks and ski groups and hikes. Mostly they loved the river.

Not long after they arrived, news of the six-dam proposal hit town. The couple joined Friends of the White Salmon River right away.

"We weren't founding members," she said. She watched closely to make sure I wrote that down. "But we did join the first year."

Everyone was fired up. They knew the truth: six new dams would reduce the wild river to a series of shallow too-warm lakes. The group's first president, Lola Carlyle, led the charge, and eventually people around the state and in Seattle and Portland jumped on the bandwagon. By the end of the decade, the proposal for six new dams had vanished, and the Friends of the White Salmon River turned its attention to Condit. The Northwest Power Planning Council was in the process of making recommendations for relicensing the dam, and the activists in Trout Lake wanted their voices heard.

Which, for Phyllis Clausen, meant attending meetings. She and Vic lived weekdays in Vancouver, and the fact that she lived in the city and spent weekends upriver proved to be an advantage. She could attend meetings in Trout Lake to hear what people *believed* was going on, and then midweek visit officials in Portland, where the headquarters for PacifiCorp, the power company that owned and operated Condit dam, were located, to find out what was *really* going on, then report back to Lola Carlyle and the others.

"So you were a spy."

"No," Phyllis chuckled. "Not a spy."

"That's a lot of meetings," I said.

"Yes, it was. And writing letters. And submitting public testimony. We were just going to do whatever we could for the river. Not for the sake of individuals or organizations. For the river."

She paused to watch me write that down: For the river.

She did not, interestingly, say: For the salmon. Salmon were the ostensible reason for the breaching. Scientists have proved, over and over, how essential they are to the ecosystem of the White Salmon River, to all the other tributaries of the Columbia, to the entire region. Tribes value them with deep spiritual fervor. But for white people, more often than not, the real fervor around dam removals is reserved for the river itself, the free river, the restored river, the seductive vision of water rushing, charging, unimpeded, untrammeled. It's fervor that stems, at least in part, from books.

There was a time when even Wallace Stegner would wax poetic about a dam. "Nobody can visit Boulder Dam itself without getting that World's Fair feeling," Stegner wrote in 1946. "It is certainly one of the world's wonders, that sweeping cliff of concrete, those impetuous elevators, the labyrinths of tunnels, the huge power stations. Everything about the dam is marked by the immense smooth efficient beauty that seems peculiarly American."

But that was before so many big dams were built so fast, before so many books exposed the problems with dams. Books like Philip Fradkin's *A River No More*, Blaine Hardin's *A River Lost*, and Mark Reisner's *Cadillac Desert* deconstructed what the authors saw as the farce of reclamation in the late twentieth century: how dam builders ignored fish and siltation and water rights in favor of harnessing for the sake of harnessing. They pilloried the subsidized waste of it all, pork barrel after pork barrel, the dirty B-side of Ross's public-mindedness.

By 1986 even Wallace Stegner had changed his tune. "The euphoria of 1946 has not lasted into the beginning of the 1980s," he wrote. He described a trip down the Colorado River in 1968, and how Lake Powell, behind the Glen Canyon Dam, was being bled to keep up the power head at Hoover Dam, how neither reservoir was anywhere near full. He didn't say he was grieving—that kind of baldness wasn't exactly Stegner's style—but you can hear it anyway. Bleeding. Bled. Dead.

In the end, the book that had once seemed the most far-fetched, Ed Abbey's 1975 novel *The Monkey Wrench Gang*, would prove the most prescient. Here, in the early years of a new millennium, dams are being obliterated by explosives right and left. And not by eco-terrorists.

In the early 1980s, the Northwest Power Planning Council determined that fish passage should be the first priority in relicensing Condit. PacifiCorp was caught by surprise. How could fish trump power? How could it realistically be expected to retrofit this old dam? The utility company dug in its heels. Fish ladders would be too expensive. Forget it.

Someone had to push back, and that job fell to Friends of the White Salmon River. In 1990, Lola Carlyle, the group's charismatic longtime president, died, and Phyllis Clausen stepped into her shoes. She reorganized the nonprofit and began talks with American Rivers.

"It wasn't just me," Clausen said. "There were other members who also contacted them."

Again, she watched me write that down. Her taste for precision, I began to realize, followed a pattern: it had mostly to do with deflecting credit. Phyllis Clausen was polite and unassuming, steely in defense of only two things: the White Salmon River and her own modesty. So she insisted, at that point, American Rivers took the reins.

American Rivers, a national organization working to protect rivers and streams, started in the early 1970s, the same heady era as Friends of the White Salmon River. Its website boasts that nearly a thousand dams have been removed in the past century in the United States—many with the organization's help—and that it has helped secure plans to remove another hundred before 2020. Back in the mid-nineties, though, most of the focus was on FERC.

The Federal Energy Regulatory Commission, formed in 1979, was the independent regulatory agency tasked with relicensing hydropower projects, which meant requiring mitigation efforts for fish or erosion or other undesirable effects. As a result, back when I was a trail crew laborer, I knew about FERC mainly as a money source. You'd be waiting to hear whether your seasonal job would be there the next year and invariably a middle manager would mention, hopefully, the possibility of getting some FERC money to bring you on. The phrase wasn't exactly accurate since FERC didn't directly dole out funds, only required the utilities to pay. Nevertheless, FERC-dictated mitigation felt from the outside, from the bottom rung of a federal land agency, like a giant cash grab. The utilities went along with the process so they could keep generating electricity, and therefore making money. Land agencies went along with it so they could glean some of that money. But American Rivers saw it differently. Some dams, it argued, didn't need mitigation. They needed removal. FERC had never actually denied a license, never even entertained the possibility. American Rivers wanted to change that.

When Phyllis Clausen contacted the group, everyone knew what was at stake. American Rivers and Friends of the White Salmon River together gathered a broad coalition of signatories—fourteen environmental groups, three federal agencies, two states, and the Yakama Nation—on a petition demanding that Condit dam be removed. The fight was on.

At one public meeting in 1993 that showed on local TV news, one you can watch on the Internet through the lens of history, schoolkids arrive carrying colorful hand-painted paper salmon. The kids march through a fluorescent-lit room, amongst a standing-room-only crowd of unsmiling spectators, until a large paper mural of Condit dam appears in the back of the room, and the kids charge through exuberantly tearing it down and pulling a blue silk "river" back through the room. You can see clearly, seventeen years after six new dams were proposed on the White Salmon River, activists had reclaimed the conversation, turned it inside out. Still, the news anchors summing up the clip in pre-commercial-break banter make this much clear: It's a cute little protest, but removing a dam? Not likely. Fantasyland.

Finally, in 1996 FERC issued an environmental impact statement that required installation of fish ladders at Condit. Everyone knew that would never happen. The estimated cost of the new measures was triple the cost of demolition, so the choice was a no-brainer. PacifiCorp had nearly two million customers in six states and no need to hang on to Condit. The company asked permission to decommission. After that, bringing down the dam should have been a cinch. But it was not.

"Why did it take so long?" I asked.

Phyllis Clausen shook her head. She couldn't say for sure.

I knew part of the reason. Klickitat and Skamania county commissioners opposed the dam removal vehemently, at some point even more than PacifiCorp itself. They sued and re-sued and even threatened to purchase the dam through condemnation.

"In all those years, did your opinion of politicians go up or down?" I asked.

Phyllis laughed.

"I learned that it's a very hard job," she said. "If you're not someone who can balance things, you're not going to get elected or get reelected. I could never do it. I'm not enough of an equivocator. Not when it comes to the river."

Did she have regrets? Sure, she said. She had regrets for the steelhead fishermen who lost their good fishing spot below the dam, for the cabin owners on Northwestern Lake who lost waterfront property.

What about for herself? What about that fifteen-year wait?

No regrets, she insisted. The wait allowed her to concentrate on other projects like securing Wild and Scenic River designation for the upper stretch of the river, designation that passed in 2005.

After a time, she no longer believed she'd live to see Condit removed, but she told herself: I'm going to push as long as I'm alive. For the sake of the river.

Is dam removal always the right answer? No. Not every dam is as flawed as Condit. Even American Rivers supports the continued operation of most hydropower projects. An undammed river will always be healthier than the same river with dams, they say—of course!—but climate change is climate change. The teacher at the dam history class had argued as much. Hydropower is clean energy, he said, contributing no greenhouse gases, and it's a better option than solar—the minerals required to make the batteries are dangerous, their removal exploitative—and a better option than wind, which damages bird and bat populations. Knee-jerk support for every dam removal strikes me as a bad case of staying wed to the conventional, sometimes wrong-minded, ideals of our own time. A liberated river, like power to the people, is an irresistible concept, an undeniably good one, but one that will almost certainly have unforeseen consequences.

Still, still, I live beside a wild river. For years on trail crew, we drove to trailheads on a rough dirt road, the landlocked Stehekin road, slowly—you couldn't go more than ten or fifteen miles per hour—beside a narrow stretch of river, translucent jade, cresting white and undulating over gray granite boulders, running amongst cedars and firs draped with lichen like emerald tinsel, populated by Harlequin ducks surfing and American dippers dipping and, in shadowy eddies, cutthroat trout lurking. I never stopped being awed by that stretch of river even when I saw it every day. I understood Phyllis Clausen's passion. She hadn't bought into a concept. She didn't liberate every single river, or just any river, she liberated the river she knows best and cares most about.

On October 26, 2011, Phyllis Clausen sat among a small group of invitees—reporters and VIPs—in white folding chairs under a tent set up for the occasion. The White Salmon River, the below-dam dregs of it, ran slow in the canyon below them and a flat-screen TV sat dark before them. They were bundled in coats and hats under propane heaters. They did not for sure know what to expect. They'd been told it could take several hours for the released water to reach them. Then it happened. They heard the explosion—and they cheered and clapped and hugged one another—and watched live video feed as water burst through a fifteen-foot gash at the base and soon, much sooner than anyone expected, charged into the channel below.

Phyllis Clausen sat beside an old friend and fellow river crusader. At the moment of the breach, he leaned over and grabbed her, his head bowed, in an emotional embrace. A newspaper photographer captured that moment. She showed me a copy of the photo to clarify one important point. The caption claimed that they were crying. They were not crying, Phyllis said. They were laughing.

After nearly two hours of interview time at the clubhouse, I worried that Phyllis Clausen was growing weary, but she was not. She had already told me how Vic died in 2007, how she'd sold the property in Trout Lake to a young couple she hoped would love it as fiercely as they had. She'd told me how rarely she gets up there anymore, though she tries, at least, to see the penstemon bloom in May, and I told her I'd like to try to go with her one day, to see the flowers and the free-flowing river. For now, she invited me to her home, not far away. She wanted to show me something, she said. We climbed into the Buick together, she in her purple coat and knit beret, and drove past plum trees in bloom, pansies and petunias in well-tended beds, lime-green moss on the tree bark, and we drove past cul-de-sacs with generic unfitting names—Fair Oaks, though there are no oaks, Baypoint, though there is no bay—and eventually some sad soggy fairways.

"It's a public golf course," she said, "not a private one." Echoes of J. D. Ross.

Inside, she offered me a seat on the sofa as she riffled through a stack of well-organized papers.

"Here it is," she said.

She handed me an issue of *Popular Mechanics* dated 1925.

She sat beside me and told me the story. Back in the 1970s, a friend had picked up a whole stack of these, and Vic was thumbing through this one at a dinner party when he stumbled upon an article describing a lift designed to take salmon up and over the Condit dam. The article had appeared six years after the last fish ladder at Condit had failed.

Phyllis urged me to open to a yellow-tab-marked page. "Elevator Saves Lives of Salmon" read the title. Thirty-five years after they discovered the magazine, nearly ninety years after its publication, the magazine was musty and worn, the illustrations elaborate and dated, but to Phyllis Clausen it held great meaning, like a talisman or an omen. Even at the end of a long rainy afternoon of talking with me, she'd known right where to find it. I skimmed to get the gist. The design did not seem unworkable, but that was not the point; the dam was now gone, or soon to be, and the salmon could swim free. I looked up and she looked directly back at me, and suddenly the point was clear. If people cared this much about the river long before Phyllis and Vic Clausen ever arrived, maybe they'd still care when they're gone.

12

She Who Watches

Bingen, Washington—April 2012

The Columbia River Gorge is scenic any time of year, but in spring it is stunning. Arrowleaf balsamroot, the ubiquitous yellow flower halfway from daisy to sunflower, brightens entire slopes. Denser green perennial species—sword ferns and salal—bunch in cliff-shaded pockets. Above it all the snowy volcanoes float—Hood, Adams, and lopsided St. Helens—and everywhere waterfalls pour down steep basalt. You'd think this is where the Cascades get their name, from the waterfalls, but it's not. They're named for the Cascade Rapids, the once-lively stretch where the river dropped forty feet in two miles and cleaved the mountain range that runs from Northern California to British Columbia. The rapids were drowned by Bonneville dam in 1937, just as Celilo Falls, the great Native fishing site where fifteen to twenty *million* salmon passed each year, was drowned by the Dalles Dam in 1957. Not far from here Tsagilalal looks down on it all.

I'd learned about Tsagilalal, She Who Watches, the most famous rock art on the Columbia Plateau, in a college class many years earlier, and I'd been fascinated ever since. Half pictograph, half petroglyph, her face is cat-like or raccoon: eyes with dark elliptical centers and concentric whorls of lightness surrounding them—lightness both painted and chipped into the red-stained stone—and ears upright and attentive. Some people say she has her tongue sticking out, but that's up for debate. In photos she appears stenciled or stamped, very large, and yes, very watchful. Legend holds that she was a chief turned to stone by Coyote (in some versions because he disapproves of women as chiefs) and charged with standing guard over the people. Tsagilalal is not ancient; she dates back only three hundred years, but those three hundred years are ones of unfathomable change. She's perched on the Washington side of the river in a spot protected from vandalism—protected as she protects—and I hoped to see her on this quick trip south, but first I had an appointment to meet Pat Arnold, the current president of Friends of the White Salmon River, so I sped down Interstate 84 on the Oregon side of the river, the faster route, alongside steady streams of Sunday tourists.

What you don't see in the Columbia Gorge—excepting the dams, big concrete exceptions—is development. Thirty years after legislation passed to protect the corridor, some of the millions of tourists who pass through each year take this fact for granted; others, veterans of the activist era, celebrate the victory; still others claim that the growth-management laws represent the first ominous steps toward one-world government. But there's no denying the effect. The flooded river, as Blaine Harden argues in *A River Lost*, may have been reduced to a bathtub, the mighty fishing grounds given over to trust-funders kite-surfing at race-car speeds, but to gaze out at the uncluttered horizon is to believe on some level that She Who Watches has been doing her job.

Admittedly, she's had some help.

It'd been more than six months since Condit dam was breached. The dramatic YouTube footage had gone viral, touted even by *National Geographic* as "spectacular." What had been a steady, slow political movement, mostly unnoticed for decades, became an overnight sensation. It was easy to see why. The footage showed water spewing forth less like the flow from a fire hydrant than like a tsunami. The rapid breach had been designed to mimic a landslide or a volcanic eruption intended to move sediment quickly downstream—by contrast the reservoirs behind the Elwha dams would be drained slowly over a three-year span—but the movement proved quicker even than expected. Northwestern Lake, the reservoir behind the dam, drained in less than an hour. Cut logs from the lake bottom shot through the fifteen-foot tunnel with tons of sediment, mostly very fine-grained sand. In the video the flow moving downstream looks gray and thick as sludge, like cement being mixed in a wheelbarrow, complete with undissolved chunks. Rapid breaches like this have taken place elsewhere, but the dams were smaller, the sediment coarser. What long-term effects to expect from this one was a matter for debate.

At home I watched the video over and over as the last roof-shed piles of snow around the house gave way to glacier lilies and trillium. In spring in Stehekin the river recedes from view as eye-level brush leafs out—vine maple, red osier dogwood, willow—and it's louder than in winter, much louder. When the first days warm up enough to open windows, you can hear it charging steadily, white noise, both a comfort and a vague threat. Vague because spring floods are not as bad as fall ones. Water seeps over the road at the base of our driveway, then runs down the road, and we drive through it until it splashes the floorboards, then we park and walk around the water or through it in rubber boots. The road relocation, on days like that, did not seem a bad idea. It was easy to forget that big change might be forthcoming, the way we might forget about wildfires during a rainy spring or floods in drought. You know it's there, know it might happen any day, but you can't worry about it.

That's how we felt ten years earlier, when the biggest big flood tore through the valley in mid-October. We'd been worried about fires for so long we'd forgotten about the possibility of a flood, and then when it came we concentrated on the cleanup around houses, and didn't realize, at first, that the biggest change had occurred upvalley. The big flood cut off thirteen upper miles of the Stehekin road, washed it to bedrock, and the Park Service would not allow reconstruction. Conservation groups chimed in gleefully. When nature reclaims a place, they argued, let it be. Re-wilding, they called it. Meanwhile, our neighbors petitioned politicians and battles raged all the way to the U.S. Congress.

Some people called it, disparagingly, the road to nowhere, and it was, literally, but it was our only road, our safety valve, our escape from small-valley fever, our way into the mountains. It was not as if we could choose to take another road. If we wanted to get to that stunning upper stretch of river or the trailheads beyond, we'd have to walk, and there are few endeavors as disheartening as walking for miles on a road you used to drive daily, and walking twenty or thirty extra miles takes time, and who gets that much time off work? I understood outsiders' opposition: Why's there a road in wilderness anyway? Why spend federal dollars on rebuilding one? But from the inside it felt like an amputation. Part of who we'd been was missing. Anyone in our shoes would've felt the same way.

I wanted to talk to Pat Arnold about the Condit dam removal because she still lived in Trout Lake, close to the fray. She said she could squeeze me in between the Democratic caucus—crucial to her not so much for the national races as for the local ones—and the annual meeting of the board of directors of Friends of the White Salmon River. A busy day. She would've preferred to take me on a hike to show me the now-undammed river, but we did not have time. Instead, she asked to meet at Solstice Pizza in Bingen (rhymes with "engine") across from Hood River, Oregon, on the Washington side. Solstice was easily the grooviest pizza joint I'd ever seen. A colorful chalkboard menu featured vegan and gluten-free choices, local beers and salad greens. Soft blues guitar played on the stereo. The crowd was loud and exuberant, diverse in age, from young families to active seniors, but homogeneous in a way, liberal and outdoorsy, which seemed odd in a small Northwest town. No one wore suspenders. No American cars besides the Buick parked in the lot. I didn't know if it was slop-over tourists from Hood River, or upscale Portland seeping east, but the economy in Bingen seemed to be thriving. I ordered iced tea and a small portabella-and-feta pie and waited.

Pat Arnold arrived moving fast and breathing heavily. She ordered pizza for the board meeting, checked her watch, slid onto a high stool, and launched into the story of how her day began with a grass fire she started by accident while burning an irrigation ditch. She had to chase it down with buckets in her ditch boots. The story amused me because Laurie starts grass fires like that in the orchard all the time, and I've spent time bucket chasing them myself, and I'd have liked to tell Pat Arnold as much, but there was not time. She had things she wanted to say. She leaned back and exuded confidence, her shoulder-length gray hair uncolored, her glasses rimless, her manner forthright. If she seemed a little bit prickly, it was a familiar kind of prickly. She treated me the way I'd treat journalists poking around Stehekin. Not standoffish but not schmoozy either. Still, it was startling to be the outsider, to hear the bristly stubbornness and the disregard for the usual environmental lines of battle.

To start with she distrusted the new green industry in town: Insitu, a drone company. The pizza place was loud so I had to ask her to repeat. Drones?

"Drones. Yes. Small surveillance aircraft."

The company—nearly the entire industry by some accounts—had moved into the area, bringing gobs of money. They'd bought up every storefront in town. Later when I'd read more, there'd be nothing but fanfare. Upscale jobs! Clean, smart industry! There is, of course, a sinister undercurrent. The company's owner had originally designed the unmanned aircraft with the best intentions—for long-range weather forecasting, or perhaps, Pat Arnold thought, for forest fire reconnaissance or backcountry rescues—but ever since the start of the Iraq war, they'd had a primarily military focus. Civilian deaths in Iraq and Afghanistan and Pakistan? The potential for civilian surveillance in the United States? These are not Pat Arnold's primary concerns. Her concern is the White Salmon River watershed, and she fears Insitu is not helping matters.

The valley remains rural, almost entirely so, with forests and orchards and vineyards. Companies like Insitu bring in people who naturally want to develop that land, especially land close to the river. Already revisions to the county growth management plan were in the works, had been in the works in fact for several years. Friends of White Salmon River stood in fierce opposition from the get-go, but it was hard to get broad support. It had tried, for example, to get American Rivers on board to no avail.

"They'd just say: Don't rock the boat. We gotta get the dam out. Don't worry about the rest of the stuff. We'll deal with it later."

It makes sense that a nationally based nonprofit would be skittish about getting involved in a rural county growth management plan. Dam removal is higher profile and closer to American Rivers' mission, for one thing. For another, despite the excruciating thirty-five-year wait, removing a dam may be easier to pull off than curbing development. After all, it's not just newcomers who support the plan, it's also people with deep family roots in the area.

"We're still doing the settler mentality," Pat Arnold said. "Many of the people who are deep into this are people who have immediate family members who moved in when the first white people moved into Trout Lake in the 1880s. We have dairy farms up there where the great-grandfathers were the first settlers."

She described the situation with surprising empathy. Much as she despises the new pro-growth policies, she doesn't hold much grudge against her rural neighbors. She believes natural resource industries like farming and logging may be the best hope for preserving the environment. What she sees on the horizon is a kind of gentrification. Even the presumed economic benefits of a free-flowing river could bring mixed blessings: higher property values, more whitewater enthusiasts and tourist dollars.

"There are 21,000 people who live in this county, and the tally of self-reported kayakers or rafters is 25,000 every year, so it's more than the county population. That's a huge pressure on the river."

Could the big national groups help with that? She'd told me they planned to stay involved. I didn't quite understand how.

"This is a major event," she said, "a huge event, and everyone is going to want to monitor progress."

I bristled at the mention of monitoring. Back home, in recent years it seemed like we'd too often see more federal money allocated for monitoring than for, say, maintaining hiking trails or growing apples. Crews are hired to monitor the spread of invasive weeds rather than yank them, monitor the effects of prescribed fires rather than set them. The contrarian in me does not believe, in the parlance of our times, it's sustainable. The more reasonable side of me knows if we don't monitor, we can't take the long view. We don't have the oral histories Native people have, we don't have the traditional knowledge, we have what's recorded on a page. Still, I bristled. Pat Arnold wanted to find ways around conflicts between paddlers and fisherman, wanted to prevent large developments with iffy water rights. Any of that could happen in a heartbeat, I thought, while someone is out carefully monitoring.

But that wasn't what bothered Pat Arnold most. Her substantial ire, the spitting mad variety, is reserved for the county commissioners whom she blames for pushing the pro-growth policies and also for the years of vehement resistance to the Condit removal.

"It really tore our community apart," she said.

The commissioners had even resisted drafting plans for salmon recovery. They simply would not discuss fish.

"Why not?"

"Because if they did they'd have to admit that Condit was coming down, and as far as they were concerned Condit was not coming out ever ever ever over their dead bodies."

In fact, at a meeting only two weeks earlier, she said, a commissioner had stood to say now that Condit had come down, the first domino has fallen, so everyone had better beware.

The domino effect is an argument few environmentalists want to touch: the lurking anguished fear among many longtime northwesterners that once one dam comes down, the rest will follow. Despite the all-or-nothing histrionics, it does not seem an entirely unreasonable fear. Besides hundreds of dams back East, more big western dams came tumbling down every year: the Elwha dams, of course, plus the Marmot Dam on the Sandy River and the Savage Rapids Dam on the Rogue. The removal of more contentious dams loomed, including the ones that dominated the news and clogged courtrooms, the four dams on the Klamath River and four more on the lower Snake. Every single online discussion, every single legislative debate, and every environmental impact statement spoke of balancing ecosystems and economies. Most cited local community needs. Many suggested rivers should be restored to a "preindustrial" state. But nothing was going back to how it was. Dams weren't going back up. Suspenders weren't coming back to Bingen. Indian culture was not going to rise up triumphant and benevolent to show white folks how to manage a river right. Pat Arnold told me she'd been hopeful when she saw the first thing the Yakama did when the decision to bring down Condit looked certain was buy property near the river. She thought maybe it'd be for science, but no, it was for enforcement, to make sure the tribe gets its proper allotment of the harvest.

"Recreational fishermen won't like that," she said.

Other members of the board of directors began to arrive. Our time was nearly up.

"I have one thing I need to tell you," she said. "The Yakama have this proposal to build a hatchery on the Klickitat River and they have big problems. Their management objective is to produce as many fish as possible for the commercial fishermen, but the wild fish people want wild fish."

"You think you'll see the same controversy on the White Salmon?"

"There's no proposal to introduce hatchery fish at this point, but when you get to talking about restoration or reclamation or whatever . . ."

She let the sentence dangle, and I waited, wondering what she saw from her perspective.

"I thought that was very interesting," she said.

What she saw was simple: this might mean trouble.

From the pizza place, it was a short drive to the confluence of the White Salmon and the Columbia, and farther upriver along a two-lane highway to the shores of Northwestern Lake, the reservoir created by Condit, the reservoir that's now drained. Warning signs greeted me at the county park: Area Closed. The former lake bottom was the color of worn ceiling tiles, the sickly off-white of dried glacial silt, and below the high-water mark: mud, mud, mud. Huge boulders lined a ramp, a raft take-out under construction, the mud freshly chewed by an excavator, and the river at the base was so narrow that you couldn't imagine how it once filled the basin. I hopped on rocks and stared into an eddy and thought I caught a flash of orange. A salmon, I thought, salmon! But it was far too early for salmon to be here, the dam was still being demolished, and months too soon for salmon to be that color anyway, the color of spawning. I looked closer to glimpse a buried scrap of safety flagging.

The land in and around the former lake belonged to PacifiCorp, always had. The cabin owners held leases, and the leases clearly indicated the possibility of dam removal, but the fate of the fifty or so cabin owners had still dominated many new stories. The county commissioners, especially, pointed to their fate as tragic and unnecessary. I'd imagined the lakeshore homes to be abandoned. I expected vacation homes, charming but rickety, like a downscale version of *On Golden Pond*, but I should have known better. These were regular homes, some with docks now jutting over nothingness. Several were inhabited. I walked along Lakeview Road with no lake in sight. No view at all. A dog on a chain barked. A mildewed pickup sat in a driveway. A few people loitered in their yards in the late afternoon sun, and every one of them scowled at me with disdain. None of the ridicule or danger you'd expect in certain urban neighborhoods. None of the faux manners you'd expect in a small town. I was clearly not the first to wander this direction trying to get closer to the blocked-off dam site where deconstruction was in full swing. I was clearly not welcome. Trees lined the road shoulder. Oaks and pine obscured views toward the former dam site, and the shores of the former lake were so steep that even after parking and ducking under another sign—No Trespassing—and half-jogging toward the former shore, I could not see around the bend. I could not yet see a thing.

Sunset colored Mount Hood pink on the horizon as I drove along the Columbia to a campground where the river-no-more had risen and smoothed behind the Dalles Dam, and into Horsethief Lake, a state park near Celilo Falls, near Wishram, the former bustling Indian center of trade that predated the Hudson's Bay by hundreds of years. A handful of trailers had taken up residence, and farther back across a wide empty lawn a few tent sites were lined up and numbered next to fences intended to block the wind. Sure enough, before the tent was up, the wind had picked up so the tall poplars swayed. On the lawn between my tent and the car lay a large pod eight inches long and an inch wide, left from the previous fall. Where the seeds inside had begun to dry, the pod was brown, but the edges still showed some green, leaving it mottled and twisted in the grass, looking exactly like a snake. Every time I passed it during my stay, I leapt in fear.

In the morning, I jogged from the campground toward a small Indian cemetery ringed with barbed wire, graves decorated with American flags, plastic flowers and sports memorabilia, faded snapshots, a Buddha statue, the Virgin Mary, piles of trinkets and color. I continued on to a place where pictograph-covered rocks had been placed along a newly paved trail alongside interpretive signs. The pictographs had been removed when the waters rose and stored in the basement of the Dalles Dam until 2003 when the Yakama Nation reclaimed them and brought them here. The threat of vandalism was severe enough that surveillance cameras had been mounted on boulders on a low bluff above them. I read the signs and admired the rock art, lovely and beguiling, but there was eeriness to the morning. No one fished on the river. No one roamed at all on a warm spring morning.

This is where She Who Watches does her watching, but I wouldn't get to see her. It was a Monday morning, and state park officials give tours only on weekends. I jogged back to the campground as the rising sun limned basalt cliffs in succession like a choreographed light show, slowed to a walk as I neared the tent, saw the snake-like pod, and leapt back, heart pounding. I caught my breath and turned one last time to look at the flat mile-wide river. Part of watching is guessing where danger lies, part is knowing where treasure lies. Sonar studies show that Celilo Falls, where salmon leapt and water roared and people gathered for at least fifteen thousand years, are still there, just under the surface. She Who Watches watches them still.

13

Bypass

Rocky Reach Dam, Columbia River, Washington—May 2012

The Homeland Security officer stopped me at the drive-through entrance booth. No one without clearance could enter before 9:00 a.m.

"But I have an appointment. I'll be late." I removed my sunglasses, looked her in the eye, and showed her my driver's license, the way I'd learned crossing the border at Tijuana frequently many years earlier, before I ever imagined having to do it in the rural Pacific Northwest.

"No one. Period," she said.

I'd returned to Rocky Reach Dam because after exploring the challenges and aftermath of a major dam removal, I was back to my original question: Is there a way to make a dam work for people and fish? Already bureaucracy threatened to thwart me.

I pulled a few feet away to wait next to an immaculate green lawn, cemetery-perfect, with a lone highway-side picnic table painted bright blue and yellow. Across the road, steep dry slopes had recently been screened to keep bighorn sheep from racing out onto the road and to keep loose rocks from shattering windshields. Cars sped past on the tail end of morning commuter hour between Chelan and Wenatchee. In the upriver distance, at the mouth of the Entiat River, a few fishing boats loitered in hazy morning sun, the water calm, the scene bucolic.

I reminded myself this was not the so-called natural state of things, this tamed-ness had been engineered, and I tried to imagine, as I had months before, where the old channel had been, where the river had run free. I couldn't.

A car pulled up to the booth, and the driver flashed a badge, grinning, and lingered making small talk with the attendant. That must be him, I thought. Had to be. I'd called Jeff Osborn, the license program coordinator for Chelan County Public Utilities District, on the phone from Vancouver, expecting a slick PR guy armed with condescension and sound bites. Instead, I'd gotten an easy two-hour primer on dam construction and fish migration. Jeff Osborn seemed yet another version of the modern-day reclaimer; neither a visionary nor an activist, he was straight talking and single-minded, with a flair for dissecting complicated systems, both mechanical and political.

I trailed his vehicle through the gate and, at the entrance to the visitor center, emptied my pockets into a plastic bowl and walked through a metal detector to meet him in person. He sat hunched over a small table on which he'd arranged documents to cover every inch, displaying them proudly like goods at a flea market. He was a large bearded man with glasses wearing a nylon PUD windbreaker, more high school science teacher than bureaucrat. The documents were well worn and tabbed with yellow Post-its.

"These are the bibles by which I exist," he said.

I'd asked him in advance if he could tell me the story of the innovative new juvenile fish bypass. I knew the contraption had substantially increased survival rates for juvenile fish trying to get past the dam on their way back out to sea, but I wondered how it came to be. I expected a tale of conflict and intrigue; instead he wanted to focus on reams of numbing syntax.

"These are the relicensing documents," he said. He held up thick photocopied packets one by one, carefully, almost lovingly, one for Rocky Reach Dam and one for Lake Chelan dam, the smaller dam thirty miles away, downlake from Stehekin. "They're good until 2052 or something like that."

He leaned in as if divulging a secret. In the late 1990s Chelan County PUD saw the writing on the wall, he said. The relicensing process for both dams was coming down the pipe, the same process that had derailed PacifiCorp at Condit and other dams around the country, and no longer could they expect a cakewalk. So they got to work. They created habitat conservation plans for the species that currently fell under the Endangered Species Act: the spring chinook, the steelhead, and the bull trout, and also for species that weren't listed but might someday be: the lamprey—an ugly prehistoric eel-like creature considered sacred by the Yakama—and the sturgeon.

"So those plans weren't required?"

"Exactly. The idea was, you know, those guys are back in D.C. We like to think local people know the environment better, so we thought: Let's try to guide our own destiny. We had to go get permission to do that, and a lot of licensees don't do that, but we thought it would be in our best interest to . . ."

". . . try to preempt anything that might come up."

"Exactly."

The plans covered everything, he said, and began the litany of topics.

"Recreation, shoreline management, fish management . . ."

"Which were the most hotly contested issues?" I interrupted.

"Recreation, shoreline management, fish management . . ." Osborn quipped. Truth was it had all been hotly contested. There'd been more than 150 public meetings, and the stakeholders—fishermen, tribes, government agencies, environmental groups, and PUD power customers, usually called, simply, "rate payers"—were as varied, and sometimes angry, as those involved with the Condit removal.

The entire situation was similar, except for one major difference: fish at Rocky Reach were not being stopped cold. In fact only a small percentage were being killed, and not on the way up—the fish ladder worked remarkably well—but on the way down. When I'd first learned about the bypass, almost a year earlier, I'd been skeptical: no way would a public utility do this out of kindness for fish. I had imagined aggressive activists and a sympathetic judge reluctantly taking their side, but I was wrong.

This process was a lot more boring than that; it was a long, slow, paper-and-meeting-burdened slog.

Osborn told me all the documents were available for download online. "If you're having trouble sleeping you can check them out," he joked, and then he turned earnest again. "Seems like we killed a lot of trees, I know, but again, these habitat conservation plans are the only ones in the nation." He handed one to me, and I flipped through the pages. Maybe I didn't seem as excited as I should have.

"Let's go outside and kick some rocks and take a look," he said.

We walked into the sun, and onto the dam itself, and he pointed out a fact that should've been clear to me for years—I drove past often enough—and certainly should have been clear to me after taking the tour, but wasn't: Rocky Reach Dam is constructed at a right angle. The power-house runs counterintuitively parallel to the stream because, in 1964, the number of generators and spillways they wanted could not fit. The river wasn't wide enough. So the entire complex is L-shaped: one part of the dam, the part we stood on, stops the water midstream and diverts it back toward the other section, the longer arm of the L, where the power generation happens. The result is that juvenile fish approach the dam and end up in what's called the "cul-de-sac"—the right-angle corner—and swim in circles trying to figure out where to go.

Now, as we approached the cul-de-sac, Osborn described the trial-and-error design process engineers went through working with a full-scale model at the University of Iowa.

"Iowa?"

Osborn nodded, grinning, eternally enthusiastic.

They tried different-sized openings.

"We had one that was really wide. The fish'd come in, they'd go, 'I don't like it. It's really dark.' They'd turn around and go out."

Another opening they tried had the opposite Goldilocks effect: too narrow. Eventually they found the size that was "just right" to get the fish herded into the bypass tunnel. He pointed toward it now, a water corridor the width of a municipal irrigation canal. They'd seduce the fish with 6,000-cubic-feet-per-second (CFS) flow created with thirty pumps working full-time to fool the fish into thinking they're still in a fast-moving river. Something about it—and Jeff's eager description—made me picture the tunnel at a coliseum through which the team charges at the start of a football game.

"Once we've got 'em, we can start draining water back out, through these screens," he said.

They'd cut the flow back to the mere 360 CFS required for fish going down the giant tube, and thereby salvage the rest for power generation. Genius. But getting fish in the tube and moving past the generators was only half the battle. Now they had to worry about where and how to spit them out. They had at least one cautionary tale to guide them.

At Bonneville dam engineers had installed an expensive bypass very similar to this one, but once it was in place, they found the fish were surviving at a 10 percent *lower* rate than if they'd risked the wild ride through the turbines. Neither the engineers nor the biologists could figure out why. So they gathered up a bunch of fish and sent them through, and when the fish popped out downstream in the tail race, Jeff Osborn and the other observers saw the problem immediately.

"It was like a trout hatchery where kids toss pellets on the surface and—pow! pow! pow!—fish come to the surface and snap them up. The water was bubbling with pikeminnow."

Pikeminnow. The non-native fish. The opportunists. The bad guys.

"So when people wonder why this bypass goes all the way across the river and downstream, it's simple," he said. "To avoid seeing all these salmon become dinner."

Osborn started his career with the Bonneville Power Administration in the 1980s and early 1990s, not long ago, but a radically different era when fishery concerns took a backseat to power production, a way back seat. Back then, his coworkers resented his work. They'd tell him his fish were screwing everything up, and he'd tell them they weren't his fish, he didn't make the rules. Finally, he decided his best defense would be to play show-and-tell. He took as many of them as he could out to a place on the river, Bermuda Bar, where they could watch chinook salmon spawning. Chinook are much larger than sockeye, the size of a small child, sometimes the size of a small adult—they can weigh up to 135 pounds—and when they go to move rocks to lay their eggs, they're moving boulders.

"They're like, 'Look, they're spawning,' and we talked about their mating displays and after a while it wasn't 'your' fish; it was 'our' fish."

Over the course of two or three years Osborn got every one of the Bonneville dam operators to go, and it made a difference.

"Nowadays," he said, "we run the river for fish and make power on the side."

I still wasn't buying it. Not entirely.

"That's because of the Endangered Species Act," I said.

"Absolutely. Absolutely. We had to wake up."

"What if the ESA were to be gutted?" The possibility of the legislation being gutted, or even repealed, did not seem out of the question. Politicians threaten to do it all the time. Constituents are pretty easily swayed by pitting the concerns of a kangaroo rat or a red-legged frog or a lamprey against those of human beings.

Well, he certainly hoped the agreements would stay, he said. They were contracts after all, and he believes in the process. He paused.

"Actually, if somebody said, 'You don't have to do this anymore, forget the bypass,' I'd probably just resign."

I'd arrived that morning skeptical of bureaucracy, but Osborn was winning me over.

He was not the first.

In the fall I'd taken a long walk up a cold stream in search of bull trout. Actually I didn't expect to see fish. I'd come to see redds—the gravel nests in which they lay eggs—because I'd been thinking about endangered fish, and I realized I knew nothing about them, really, so I called the Forest Service, and next thing you know I stood at a trailhead with waders in my pack and a broomstick in my hand.

"Fall feels like stream survey season," one companion announced as four of us, all women, cinched pack straps and retied boots. "Doesn't it?"

I didn't know, I said. I'd never done one. She told me she was a volunteer like me. Normally she worked as a biologist for another agency, and for this, she took the day off.

"You're in for a treat," she said.

This much I know about federal land managers: they're often desk-shackled, mired in paperwork and politics, an endless cycle of public meetings and setbacks and revisions. They're people who love the outdoors but whose careers, over time, have grown less and less like Aldo Leopold's and more and more like that of the title character in Kurosawa's *Ikiru*, the desperate entrenched bureaucrat trying to make meaning of a life of repetition. One way to make meaning, or at least find some relief, is to find a way to go outside. These women had.

So I was impressed. I was also concerned. When I signed up, I pictured a stroll along a stream bank. The waders, the broomstick—striped with colored depth markers—and the overstuffed day packs disabused me of that notion.

"We'll walk how far?" I asked. "A couple miles?"

"Hours," another woman replied. "We'll be in the water for four or five hours."

The group leader, Cindy Raekes, paired me with herself and announced that we'd take a lower, easier stretch of creek. We hiked at a steady clip, and then stopped at a small side channel.

"This is us," she said.

We dropped down through patches of head-high devil's club—the ubiquitous Northwest shrub with half-inch spines on its stems—clambered over fallen old-growth cedars, waded through deep pools. Should a zoo or a nature preserve try to re-create a healthy mid-elevation forest like this, they'd never get it right. Moss so thick, logs this weathered and wedged, you can't fake it. As we walked, Cindy explained the surveys. They do them each fall on three tributaries—"tribs," she calls them—and she's been doing them for twenty years.

"Twenty years?"

She nodded and kept moving.

Bull trout, she explained, are less romanticized than salmon—maybe it's the name?—but they're the choosiest of salmonoid species. They want the coldest cleanest water, the least manipulated stream banks, the most intact forests. Prima donnas, you might say, or else savvy customers.

We reached the main trib, and Cindy forged ahead, never breaking stride. I stumbled behind through thigh-deep water, leaning hard on the now-essential broomstick.

The rocks on the bottom ranged in earth tones from rust to orange, with quartz veins glittering white. Where the rocks were polished clean— no dirt, no algae—that's where we looked. There the fish dig a shallow depression, lay eggs, then cover them with rocks the size of a toddler's fist: the redd. After an hour or so, at last, I began to see the redds clearly. We'd hang a flag on a nearby limb and label them: possible, probable, definite.

Then they appeared. A spawning pair in a wide shallow swath. The male eased beside the female, more snuggle than thrust, and the female flipped on her back to expose a silver belly and writhed, and I gasped. What part of the sex act, I wondered, was this?

"She's working," Cindy said. "That's how she cleans the rocks."

On cue, the male joined the frenzy, and together they did a little housework.

Cindy sat watching, nearly giddy, in silence.

There are days that make work worth it: when a teacher hears a kid spell aloud, when a mason fits a corner tight, when a musician hits the right note. Back home when I'd try to describe the scene in the creek—like prayer, I'd say—I'd picture Cindy, too, and the way, when we caught up with the others, they buzzed with excitement. Their day of work had been worth it.

Back at Rocky Reach, I asked Jeff Osborn about the Boldt decision, the Supreme Court decision that gave half of the salmon harvest back to Native Americans.

"Will the contention never subside?"

"I think it's gone beyond that," he said. "The Boldt decision forced managers to actually manage and they've been doing a much better job, but now it's getting into hatcheries versus wild fish and your four Hs—

hatcheries, harvest, habitat, hydropower—and generally, since I'm hydro, I want the other three to fix the problem but don't touch my H. Where's that balance? Ask twenty-five different people, get twenty-five different answers. That's where we have to start."

Finally, I understood. There's no way to bypass the bureaucracy because there's no way to bypass the conflict. In the end, it seemed possible—if not particularly palatable—that the bureaucracy is, in fact, the way through. Taking into account many human perspectives is, perhaps, the only way to make things right, or as right as possible.

To say the day at Rocky Reach was as satisfying as the day of the bull trout survey would be overstatement at best. There's something crucial still, always, about doing work outside—hands dirty, waders in the creek—and nothing underscores our cultural disconnect from nature better, or worse, than land managers who have to take a vacation day to work outside on the lands they manage. But in a way Jeff Osborn's meetings-and-paperwork made that lovely survey day possible. The wild bull trout depend on the good management of the dams. Something in the trade-off reminded me of those bumper stickers: "If you value your freedom, thank a soldier." I'd always bristled because in my most idealistic moments I want to believe we could have a free world without soldiers. But I know we couldn't. On the other hand, I'd been heartened to discover that soldiers are so often, though not always, strong, skilled, and earnest people. Ditto for bureaucrats. Easy to dismiss dam employees and the fish counters as tools of the machine, harder to see them as the keepers of the ever-tenuous peace.

We gazed upriver together for a moment, and I remembered I had one more question for him.

"Where was the old channel?"

"Oh," Jeff pointed, "it was right up there against the north bank."

Now I knew. Just like that. I could picture it clearly: the deep blue churn against the dry hills, white water dropping fast. The answer satisfied my curiosity but did not offer the flight of imagination I'd hoped for, transport to some mythical landscape of hope in need of restoration. More than anything, the knowledge felt like trivia. The flat water was boring, yes, the concrete ugly, the guards infuriating. But this was the world I'd inherited. Every single dam on the Columbia existed before I did, as did the pervasive reactionary longing for the time before they did, a longing I sometimes feel myself. But the lesson I kept relearning about reclaiming is that it's not about what we've lost, how to retrieve or re-create it, but how best to move forward.

"Thank you," I said.

Jeff Osborn shook my hand and walked off to make small talk with the bored Homeland Security guards at the entrance. He set down his armload of documents carefully on the counter, keeping them close.

14

Restored . . . Salvaged

Hood River, Oregon—November 2012

Aphone call changed everything. I sat in the front seat of the Buick with the door ajar in a parking lot flooded with winter sun, stunned. I had not seen it coming.

I'd planned to raft the White Salmon River. I'd brought rubber boots and long johns and neoprene gloves—it was after Thanksgiving after all—in hopes of joining the first commercial trip to run the narrow lower gorge where Condit dam used to be. I'd been corresponding for months with Mark Zoller, whose family has run the above-the-dam stretches of the White Salmon for three generations, but the date the river would open—the date when the final remnants of Condit would be out of the water—kept getting pushed back. I'd rearrange plans and rearrange them again, growing more and more frustrated, more and more annoyed, but I knew it wasn't Mark's fault, not anyone's fault really, just the nature of the work. A single blast does not remove a dam.

You could watch the progress on a video blog, *White Salmon Restored: A Timelapse Project*. Local watershed expert Steve Stampfli teamed up with young Portland filmmaker Andy Maser to set up two remote cameras at the exact spot where cameras had documented dam construction a hundred years earlier. They planned to document the removal, which was not, by any standard, going to be easy. After the initial blast, explosives were out since it would be impossible to salvage the debris—35,000 cubic yards of concrete—that would end up downstream and wreak havoc on aquatic habitat. Instead, giant tracked jackhammers crept atop the dam breaking off chunks of concrete and worked in concert with excavators that pinched the chunks in steel clamshell claws and set them in dump trucks. This video, the kind that might appeal to six-year-old boys, captivated me for hours. I've done enough labor to know how difficult this work is, how there can be a kind of grace to the ear-splitting creak of an eight-ton machine on tracks atop a strip of concrete over a narrow river. As the dam lowered, work was squeezed into an even narrower rock channel at the base and became more difficult yet. So the date kept getting pushed back.

Finally, Mark Zoller wrote in late October with the news that he'd gone down the lower gorge in a kayak. It was great, he claimed, amazing. He sounded breathless with excitement even via email. Now, at last, everything was set. Except. The first trip would fall on the day I'd planned to spend with family for the holidays.

Could he wait one week? I asked. He could.

But winter couldn't.

While I was out of state, torrential rains descended. The White Salmon River rose to flood stage, and who knew how long it would stay there? Mark needed to take a long-planned off-season vacation, and long johns in my luggage notwithstanding, things were not looking good.

Still, I'd planned to meet Steve Stampfli in person, so I headed to the Gorge, and all along the way, I thought about symmetry: the young fruit trees in rows wrapped in white rodent protectors, the white flashes of magpie wings, the pressure-treated posts on guardrails that mirror the vertical columnar basalt against the sky, the geese in flight in trademark Vs, the scruff of poplars on a ridgetop, power poles of sun-darkened cedar, and train tracks shining bright as ice. It's easy, sometimes, to bemoan the fact that humans like to impose order—whatever order we deem necessary, at any cost—but nature has order, too, and maybe the effort is necessary, every bit of it, to balance entropy.

Which seemed equally in evidence. Along the river, a hand-painted sign advertised elk jerky and smoked cheese in front of a season-shuttered trailer. Rotted fence posts leaned under the weight of barbed wire heavy with blackberry vines draped like beards. Across from the train trestle at the mouth of the White Salmon a lone snow goose and a family with a toddler stood on mudflats. I'd read concerns about turbidity, the dramatic loss of water quality due to dam-held sediment now being flushed downstream. PacifiCorp had been granted a temporary waiver from Clean Water Act regulations. I stood on the road bridge as the sun dropped low in the south looking down at the water—flood brown, nearly opaque, turbid indeed—rushing past the place where the toddler dragged a stick through the mud, and I wondered, apart from floods, how old that child might be before the water once again ran clear.

I rented a cheap room at a hostel in the small town of White Salmon, an amenity available because of the influx of international windsurfers to the Gorge in warmer months. The place was clean and colorful, affordable, and, in the off-season, uncrowded. In the morning, I sat on my assigned bunk watching morning rain trace patterns on a street-facing window and called a spokesperson for PacifiCorp. I had a handful of questions about the loss of power generation, about the plans for revegetation at the site. The spokesperson answered with sound bites. Power loss? Every windmill has the potential to produce 2 megawatts of power; a half dozen of them equals Condit. Revegetation? Grass seed had been spread in the fall and trees would follow in spring. I may as well have been speaking with the script-reading tech-help guy in a distant call center. I tried to make headway, to get at the human heart. What was his job exactly? He was one of three full-time employees doing public relations for PacifiCorp on the Condit removal. What had he studied? Marketing. Shaping the story had now co-opted the story, here as everywhere else. I wondered how many tree planters might be hired for the cost of three full-time PR salaries or what the combined talents of three clever marketing majors could do for, say, getting dams removed from the Klamath River or the Snake. I knew I was being unrealistic. There was nothing wrong with the guy or what he'd told me. There was only me with my too-big ideas and my rundown Buick.

I left the hostel, bought coffee at a drive-through stand, and drove a steel toll bridge across the Columbia and through the tidy upscale town of Hood River, the windsurfing mecca, to Steve Stampfli's office in a yellow-shingled house at the Oregon State University experimental station amongst acres of dew-wet orchards. From the parking lot, I marveled at how this low rise above town split the horizon precisely in half between Mount Adams to the north and Mount Hood to the west.

Stampfli is a tall man, strong jawed, with thick gray hair you could easily imagine as once-blond, befitting a windsurfer, and a slow drawl. He began every reply, once it came, with a lilting drawn-out "Well . . ."

I'd read that Stampfli started his career in mine reclamation, so I asked him right away about the difference between restoration and reclamation.

"Well . . . I think restoration really connotes returning to original condition," he began.

"That's the question, right? What's the original condition? Is there such a thing?"

He stopped cold, offended maybe or simply knocked off balance. I made a mental note to ask him again, but for now I told myself to keep my trap shut and let the man tell his story, and with a little urging he did.

He'd been working at a gold mine in the Black Hills of South Dakota in the 1980s—a big leach operation that "definitely had the capacity to do a lot of harm"—doing what he could to mitigate damage, when one year he decided to chuck it all. He packed up and moved to Hood River, lured by the windsurfing. Within a year he went to work for the local conservation district along the White Salmon during the long Condit battle. He did not take sides back then. He couldn't. His employer, the conservation district board, was, by nature, conservative, as such boards tend to be, and he had a job to do: protect streams and water quality.

"I did help out with some of the early prescriptions for revegetation, but we also didn't go out and rally for dam removal, even though at the same time we were preparing for restoration of fish populations and really wanted it to happen, but . . ."

"You couldn't be an activist."

"Exactly."

After he retired in 2002, he got more involved. He worked a year with AmeriCorps at a fish hatchery along the Columbia, a job that involved educating the public on the Condit dam removal, getting people used to the idea. That's where he discovered the historic photos that opened the door to his time-lapse photography project.

I asked about a particular blog post that had piqued my interest, one in which he lobbied for using "tried and true" methods of reforestation. "Local foresters and nurserymen have, for the past fifty years, developed proven methods of reestablishing forests," he wrote. It would behoove the current contractors to use those methods, he implied. The tone was distinct from that of other posts: a little proud, a little defensive. Maybe it resonated with me because of the way local knowledge in Stehekin so often trumps that brought in by so-called experts. Was that what he meant?

"Well . . . when companies go out and devise site restoration plans, they typically go to consultants like landscape architecture firms with a real . . ." He paused. "Maybe it's an urban focus."

Consultants might specify three-gallon pots of some generic species—red osier dogwood, say, or vine maple—to be purchased downtown and planted. But they would not specify a seed source. Local timber companies, by contrast, learned long ago to stick with native seeds and stock for better results.

"You can't necessarily see it immediately," he said, "but with pine and fir a non-local seedling might grow okay at first then after five years it might not perform as well."

I thought about traditional ecological knowledge and how Steve Stampfli was advocating a modern-day version of this in a way: the TEK of logging companies. The irony tickled me, and also made me wonder what Stampfli thought of the tribes involved, if he'd worked with them. Not a lot, he admitted, but he admired the work they did and was optimistic about their role.

"I hope the Yakamas exert their historic right to fish and to erect scaffolds on the river."

I pictured the iconic photos from Celilo Falls where Indians perch on rickety stick-framed platforms anchored to the rocky shore and maneuver long-handled nets into the wild churn. In some they hold chinook salmon aloft for the photograph with a thumb and middle finger through the fish's jaw, casual as hauling a plastic grocery sack.

"That would be cool," I said.

Steve Stampfli laughed.

"It would," he said. "It sure would."

The conversation meandered. He described another PacifiCorp dam removal he'd been working on lately, the smaller PowerDale Dam on the Hood River. It's a complicated project, one that involves taking mitigation money from the controversial Columbia River Crossing—the proposed construction of a new I-5 bridge between Portland and Vancouver—to fund restoration of wetlands sixty miles to the east. Precisely the kind of deal that sours some people on the whole concept. Which brought me back to my original question.

"So, what do you see as the difference between restoration and reclamation?"

"Well . . . twenty years ago we'd say we worked in reclamation. Now we say we work in restoration even though we really don't. Restoration is bringing things back to pre-aboriginal state, but in practice whatever we do we have future use in mind. But I also think with future use, we're realizing the value of things like native species."

To Steve Stampfli restoration was, simply, the most recent stop on the swinging pendulum of terminology. I appreciated his honesty and his idealism, too, his belief in the idea that what's good for the land might be good for people too. But the concept still bothered me more than it bothered him. The idea of restoring a "pre-aboriginal" state, a step beyond a "preindustrial" state, an imaginary unmanipulated peopleless state of nature, devalues the very kinds of contributions Stampli is making, and devalues the traditional ecological knowledge of aboriginal people, too. Aren't we better off considering, always, changes humans have made in the past, for better as well as for worse, when considering ones to make in the future?

Before I left, we watched again the video of the breach at Condit. What had, the day before, seemed to me like a too-slow and perhaps insoluble problem—how to move a century's worth of sediment—struck this expert as success. The rapid flush allowed the water to do its own work instead of, say, bringing in heavy machinery to re-create the river channel. He narrated the draining of Northwestern Lake with the excitement of a color commentator at the big game, banks calving and sloughs reopening, water swirling in eddies, and as we watched, I felt a kind of settledness, hopefulness even, something I hadn't often felt on my travels.

I left the small map-crowded office and stepped outside into the parking lot, where fragile sunlight seemed to bode the arrival of winter. I sat in the car, door ajar, and called to check once more with the Zollers. Any chance of a raft trip? None. Whitewater enthusiasts with more skill and stake than I were already riding rapids and naming them new: Steelhead Falls, Jaws, the Raceway. I didn't need that kind of thrill. I hadn't needed to come after all, but I was glad I did. There was closure in it, less triumph than denouement, the changes from here on out would take time, like silt settling to the depths.

Then I decided to make one last call.

I'd last been in touch with Beverly Ogle in August when my long-awaited trip to Humbug Valley—for a so-called Girls Night Out camp-out—was thwarted by a wildfire. (This seemed to be a recurring thematic thread in my research as in my life: fire, flood, fire, flood.) But I'd read that the Maidu might take title to the land as soon as January, so I wondered if she'd have news. She answered the phone and took a minute to remember who I was. I'd sent her cherries in summer? I'd visited in spring? Oh, yes. Now she remembered. And, yes, she had a story. But not the kind I'd been expecting.

She'd headed up to Humbug Valley in late October in her Ford Windstar van, leading a crew that would build a fence to protect some sacred sites. The project was one of many the Maidu had completed to prove to the stewardship council that they were worthy to take over the land. They'd worked on eradicating noxious weeds, designed an interpretive kiosk. Now the fence. She was eager and hopeful, and mostly attending to the business at hand: making sure the crew knew how to get there and what to do. The day was lovely, the Chips fire, which had eventually burned 75,000 acres in the Feather River watershed, had smoldered away at last.

She came around a corner and could not believe her eyes. A full-scale logging operation was in progress. PG&E had acquired an emergency permit from the state to salvage logs from areas affected by the fire. It was logging, supposedly, to salvage trees before they gave way to rot or bugs. But, in Humbug Valley at least, this seemed a ruse.

"Most of those trees weren't burned bad. Many weren't even singed," Beverly said.

She got out of her car and went directly up to the PG&E archaeologist and the forester, people she'd known for years. They'd worked together before the prospect of land reclamation even arose, way back when Ogle worked as campground host and showed them her ancestors' graves. Now they'd done this?

"Why didn't you contact us? The Maidu Summit or the Susanville Rancheria or anyone?" I could imagine how her voice must have sounded: stern and steady, angry perhaps, but unwavering.

They told her they'd sent out the required notices. Of course, they had. They sent them via snail mail on a Friday. Today was Monday, and the logging was in full swing. No way could the notices have reached them in time. She could see trees falling across an ancient trail, and skidders—heavy tracked machines—working dangerously close to a grinding stone, a slab of granite pocked with fist-sized holes worn by generations of Maidu women using stones to grind acorns into paste. Anyone could see it. Anyone would know its importance.

"I suggest that you halt operations," she said.

The forester and the archaeologist did not respond.

Beverly got in her van and left. She called Lorena Gorbet and Farrell Cunningham and others from the Maidu Summit Consortium. The next day Lorena went up and took photos. Later I'd pull them up online. In them you could see clearly through a windshield the yellow arm of an excavator at work piling slash. The same machine that had seemed graceful on Steve Stampfli's website suddenly seemed menacing.

PG&E did not, of course, halt operations. The logging continued until they'd cut every last tree on that 218-acre hillside, avoiding only the archaeological sites that appeared on their own maps, maps made haphazardly, by all reports, in the 1980s. One hundred and fifty acres remained to be cut in a non-adjacent plot to the south in Humbug Valley, but by the time snow flew, not long before I spoke with Beverly, the operation had gleaned a smooth $500,000.

I thanked her for telling me the story and promised to be in touch. I felt duped, shaken to the core. There was nothing slow about what PG&E had done, nothing respectful. The lessons I'd learned about reclamation apparently applied only where profit didn't play. The reclaimers I'd admired most were not collecting a paycheck of any kind: Beverly Ogle, Pauline Esteves, Phyllis Clausen. The well-intentioned bureaucrats, Wade McMaster, Steve Stampfli, and Jeff Osborn, were collecting from the collective. None of what they did or said or how I interpreted it could hold up against this one cold fact: Possession is nine-tenths of the law. It didn't matter that judges had decreed more than a decade earlier that PG&E must relinquish Humbug Valley or that the salvage logging was a transparent attempt to milk every drop of profit before doing so. It only mattered that on paper Humbug Valley still belonged to PG&E.

By the time I arrived home, I knew that I could no longer be an impartial observer, if I'd ever been one. I'd have to do something about what had happened in Humbug Valley. I told anyone who would listen. I penned op-eds and sent them to dozens of newspapers, including the *New York Times*. I wrote essays and sent them to magazines, some where I knew editors well. Not one publication responded. The story made it as far as Sacramento and Chico, but no farther. I grew frustrated, nearly apoplectic. This was not right.

A thoughtful friend tried to empathize. "I've never failed to be impressed by the sheer mendaciousness of corporations when it comes to profit," he said.

I knew what he meant: This is the way it is.

And I knew what he thought, since I'd thought it myself: My outrage stemmed from naïveté. This naïveté, this faith that happy endings are deserved—that reclamation inevitably leads to triumph even if it takes a long time—seemed as shameful and as distinctly American as the wholesale greed that had exposed it.

After a discouraging month, I called Beverly Ogle again, this time from Stehekin, from the lone public phone in a dirty outdoor booth with a lousy satellite connection that stuttered and echoed and sometimes cut out. The poor connection didn't faze Beverly a bit.

They'd held a meeting with the Plumas County Board of Supervisors, which holds jurisdiction over what happens on private lands, and the meeting went well, she said. They were hoping for some kind of restitution or at least recrimination. They were still hoping to reclaim the land and, meanwhile, they needed to start tending to it. They needed to put straw on the hillsides, for starters, she said, to prevent erosion. They needed to replant. She told me she was angry, but she didn't sound angry. She told me she was sad, but she didn't sound sad.

I sat and watched cold wind kick up whitecaps on Lake Chelan, holding a pen in my shaking hand and notebook in my lap, and felt rightly chastened.

What happened in Humbug Valley seemed to me the worst outcome imaginable. But the people who were once called Diggers, they've seen worse. The traditional knowledge they hold goes way beyond ecological; it's about how to survive in a world of grief. You confront when you need to confront. You stare clear-eyed into the past and into the future. You don't overestimate what you can do. (The *New York Times*?) You don't underestimate either.

"What would've happened," Beverly asked me, "if I hadn't showed up that day?"

Part of me thought: Same damned thing.

Part of me thought: The truth would never have been told.

There'd be a healing ceremony in spring, she said. She'd be in touch.

15

Hope without Hope

Humbug Valley, California—June 2013

Humbug Valley was not easy to reach. In early summer, I flew to Reno, rented a car—we'd sold the Buick at last—spent the night with friends, and in the morning drove toward the Sierras as white clouds floated in the sky like the painted backdrop in a western and wildflowers speckled green foothills and snow lingered on the peaks and construction backed up traffic for miles. It'd be a long trip, and I wasn't sure how to get where I was going, but Beverly Ogle had invited me to a healing ceremony, and I did not intend to miss it.

Even the receptionist at the ranger station in nearby Chester didn't know the route for sure, though she'd been there as a kid and remembered the soda springs with nostalgia. We checked the fifteen-minute topographic maps and then the seven-and-a-half-minute maps. In each, Humbug Valley lay at the juncture of three corners: upper right, lower right, upper left. You'd have to buy them all, she said apologetically, and paste them together. I bought a forest map, a too-big map with details too small, and headed out. I stopped for watermelon and some ice, a meager potluck contribution, and drove past Lake Almanor, the drowned Maidu valley now a clear blue reservoir reflecting Mount Lassen in the distance.

Not far out of town I turned off the highway and followed logging roads that branched at intersections marked by flimsy brush-hidden posts with four-digit Forest Service road numbers or more often by paper plates marked with Sharpies or crayons with first names and arrows. The roads were rutted and washboarded, ungraveled and twisty, the trees dense enough to shade blind curves and obscure the landscape. Tall peaks? Creek ahead? How could you know? The trees were as thick as my arm is long, the bark sun-stained orange. The day was windows-rolled-down hot, and classic rock on the rental car radio blared loud—Van Halen, Foreigner, Blue Oyster Cult, and, finally, AC/DC's "Dirty Deeds Done Dirt Cheap."

This, at last, was the place. I parked beside the soda springs. On one side of the road a spring-green meadow stretched to pine-fringed ridges and beyond. On the other: a brown stubbled slope with stumps black and not-black and slash—discarded trunks with telltale green needles—piled high. The postcard invitation Beverly had sent showed this view exactly: the forested hillside as it looked before, separated diagonally by a fierce red divide from how it looks now. In person it was even more disconcerting. Don't get me wrong. A clear-cut alone can't shock me after two decades in the Pacific Northwest, but this one, with its sloppy skid marks, oversized piles of green-needled slash, seemed wasteful or worse. Pink flagging fluttered around what I assumed to be archaeological sites. Some flags were wrapped around fresh stumps smack in the middle of the cut-over area. A dozen vultures circled overhead, so I walked out into knee-high grass to find what they were after, a half-deer carcass with the head still intact, one glassy eye bulging. A cougar kill by the looks of the tidy gut pile nearby, covered entirely by flies.

A mile up the road I reached Yellow Creek Campground, nine undeveloped campsites—with running water from ground spigots but no showers or flush toilets—nestled among tall pines run by a concessionaire for PG&E and watched over by a new campground host. The place was silent. The only indication of the planned ceremony was one site, the best one, closest to the creek, reserved by a bear skin draped over a picnic table. The rules posted on the bulletin board clearly stated that saving sites was prohibited, but I was glad to see this particular violation had been overlooked. I set up my small tent and ate jerky by the creek and listened to the sounds of bugs and birds and burbling water. The valley seemed soft: grasses in shades of green-yellow and some seed heads turned auburn. The different heights, too, made the grass wavy and textured and unbroken for several miles except for the willows along the creek.

Noisy campers arrived late in the night, and I was awakened at dawn by the sound of thrushes and grouse and the strangest-sounding elk I'd ever heard. The call seemed more pathetic than majestic, and this did not seem like elk country, but I heard it over and over, until I was wide awake. Usually I jog in the morning, but I'd not planned to since there wasn't a shower in the campground and I wanted to look half-respectable, not sweaty, but I couldn't just lie on the ground thinking about the clear-cut and the ceremony to come. Jogging is the only way that I know how to pray, and prayers seemed in order.

I ran alongside the new split-cedar fence, the construction of which had brought Beverly Ogle to the valley in fall just in time to catch the logging in progress. Weathered rails set upon rocks, lupine waving beside them. I peeled off my coat and hung it on the fence and ran on. I prayed for strength and openness. I ran past the pink flags waving and toward the soda springs, where a woman in a tie-dyed shirt and a tall ponytailed man with a handlebar mustache and a striped western shirt stood. They turned out to be two of Beverly Ogle's kids, Brenda Heard-Duncan and Fred Mankins, prepping for the ceremony: hanging a tribal banner, laying out the bear skin I'd seen in the campground, and setting up a tent awning for shade. I introduced myself, and they told me they'd been expecting me, and I told them how sorry I was about what had happened.

"It's not what was done, but how," Fred said.

Fred Mankins was a logger himself, an independent contractor for thirty-five years. Even he would've salvaged the worst damaged timber, he said. But he would never log like this. Never. He pointed out the erosion along the skid trails. He would've used a highline to yard the logs out without disturbing the soil. And he wouldn't have cut everything. He would've been selective. The Forest Service owns adjacent property that burned much hotter than this, he said, and it chose to let the trees live. Even black bark can be superficial, deceptive, you know? Even if it's black fifteen to twenty feet up the trunk, you can slip a pocket knife under the bark to know if the cambium is still alive and schlepping water upwards. In nearly all of those trees, it is. Or it was.

"These trees would've been just fine," Fred said, shaking his head.

Fire has been a regular part of life here; several homes and hotels burned down over the years. He pointed out a hillside across the valley that was damaged by the Storrie fire, a fifty-thousand-acre mega-fire back in 2000, but left to recover on its own. You could see the trees coming back, amidst the silver snags.

"That's how this ought to look," Brenda said.

For this job PG&E hired a gyppo outfit, a cheap company, to get the job done fast. To do it right would've cost a little more. Fred started to guesstimate how much per acre.

Brenda interrupted him. "They don't care."

"They don't," Fred said. He sighed. "See that flagging?"

He'd put it up to mark archaeological sites, some that had been avoided, some that had not. There were Maidu house sites and milling stones, and damage had been done. He knew the PG&E archaeologist personally; he was a good guy.

"But they claimed to have surveyed the area before the logging, and they had not." He paused and kicked a boot toe in the dirt. "Besides he has no power."

The sun now hit the hillside directly, and the smell reiterated the view: fresh needles and charred earth mingled with dew-wet grass. A car approached in the distance, and Brenda wondered if it was Beverly; she hadn't yet arrived. As we squinted into the morning sun, I noticed a fenced area across the way, a small ranch.

"Are those cows?" I asked.

Brenda and Fred looked at me in unison. Well, yeah. Duh.

I told them about the odd-sounding elk I'd heard at dawn, and we laughed. The car passed; it wasn't Beverly. There wasn't much else that needed to be done to prepare, so I began to jog away.

"Check this out," Fred called. He pointed to an eave on the shelter over the soda springs.

"Barn swallows," Brenda said.

We stood together, me on my tiptoes, and watched three beaks emerge from the nest.

Back at camp I splashed off some sweat in the camp spigot and changed clothes, and by the time I returned to the soda springs, hitching a ride with Fred and Brenda in the crowded cab of their pickup, the road was lined on either side with vehicles. A large crowd mingled: young and old, Indian and white, a Mexican flute maker from Oakland, a Forest Service employee in uniform, an African American woman I recognized as a scholar and activist and longtime supporter of the Maidu. Her young son wore an NFL jersey and held a drum in his stroller.

Beverly Ogle had arrived and sat under an awning with elders and friends. A minor flurry erupted when a reporter from the *Sacramento Bee* informed her that PG&E had decided not to log the remaining 150 acres in the contract. They didn't like the bad publicity.

"It should've happened a long time before now," Beverly said.

I waited for the excitement to ebb, then went to greet her and to meet Lorena Gorbet, too, the woman I'd spoken with more than a year earlier. She looked two decades younger than her sixty-five years and hauled a drum as big around as the firs that once stood across the road. As Lorena set up the drum, and I tried to help though she needed none, two gray-ponytailed men in T-shirts, representatives of neighboring tribes, began the slow process of starting a fire by hand using a thin straight elderberry twig and two small wedges of cedar. They cut a small triangular notch in one cedar wedge and set it atop the other. Then they began taking turns spinning the elderberry madly between their palms, hands slipping down the twig. The friction created tiny embers, like cigarette ash, that collected in the notch. One of the men braced the cedar wedge under his foot, and after a while, he removed his tennis shoe and sock, so he held the wedge barefoot.

"Why did you take off your shoe?" an onlooker asked.

"To be in touch with the earth," the fire maker said. "Everyone else is just watching, but I am in prayer."

Half an hour passed before there were enough embers to put on a bed of wispy curled tinder, a double handful like an airy nest, and the two men were able to blow it to life. They set the tinder with kindling in a metal fire pit in the center of the parking lot. And the whole setting turned holy. I grew up Catholic, and though I'd left the dogma and the institution behind, ritual always moved me. Now the pungent fire conjured the spicy incense burned at my father's funeral, and the sounds of prayers in unfamiliar languages echoed Latin litanies, and something inside me stilled.

Beverly walked to the center of the circle to read from loose-leaf paper.

"We are gathered here today in a good way to ask forgiveness from this land for this man-made destruction. Today we pray to Creator to bring back the trees and native plants, grasses, animals, and birds. Everything out here is connected with the lives of our Maidu ancestors."

One of the fire makers approached each guest in the circle, waved a smudge of sunflower root like incense and with a hawk wing flung away the smoke and with it any malingering spirits. The other followed with a tobacco pipe from which he blew smoke, head to toe, then touched each person's chest flat-palmed and said "blessed person" before touching his own the same way.

As he did, Beverly continued to read her speech, slowly and loud, her tone resigned and beseeching and unwavering. She thanked everyone for coming and for what they brought—the fire, the flute, the prayers, and the wild tobacco seed that would be spread on the clear-cut slope.

"This destruction of my paradise saddens me and it's almost unbearable. The red-tailed hawk has appeared before me to share my sadness," she concluded. "We ask Creator to give us strength through prayer."

Farrell Cunningham stood and walked slowly toward the microphone. I'd known about Farrell for months: he was the chairman of the Maidu Summit, a teacher and a native plant enthusiast, and at thirty-seven one of the last fluent speakers of the Maidu language, but in person he was more humble and unassuming than I'd expected. He wore brown jeans and a plain black T-shirt, work boots and a well-worn leather driving cap—a nod perhaps to the Welsh half of his heritage—that shaded his heavy brow. A scruff of beard showed hints of gray. His voice was soft and clear as he explained that he wanted to offer a prayer in Maidu but that first all recording devices should be shut off. He would not translate, he said, but the crowd would sense the meaning. Then he spoke, addressing his prayer to the fire and the sky and the ravaged hillside in a rolling soft-voweled language and a voice both tuneful and sad, with a resonance that called to mind Gregorian chant.

Then he sat, and his sister Trina stood. Her voice was as soft as Farrell's, her presence as formidable. She sang a song she'd composed in these mountains. She'd climbed a hill and sat until it came to her, a wordless song, high-pitched, like a cry or a whistle or the wind, and then she, too, prayed.

"For all nations," she began.

I expected an "It's a Small World" litany with the nations of Europe, Asia, South America. Instead, she listed nearby tribes—Wintu, Pit River, Wailaki, Yuki—then the tribes of the Great Plains and the Southwest, a long list of names familiar and unfamiliar. She concluded by praying for all the indigenous people of the world.

"Which is," she said, "all of us."

I'd never thought of it that way.

"Find your place," she said, "and protect it."

I started to cry. If the sounds and smells were those of Catholic Mass, the sentiments ran deeper. It wasn't just about our connection with and responsibility toward one another or toward the Creator but to the land itself. Not some Edenic picture-bible version of nature, but real dusty damaged land, living and dying and nurturing us while we nurture it. Another singer sang in Maidu in a deep resonant tone, animal-like and foreign, like throat singing, more command than plea, and accompanied himself with a clapper stick. The flute maker played his elderberry flute. And still I wept. Later I'd say the ceremony had been the most spiritual of my life, but right then, I wasn't thinking that way. I wasn't thinking at all. If there is a suitable word for how I felt, it's the same one, I think, that described everyone there. Present.

At last one fire maker stood with the native tobacco he'd brought: a large bag of seed and two live plants. Members of the tribe carried handfuls of seed up the clearcut hillside to plant, not as a crop, but as a healing gesture before the reforestation to come, and the rest of us, in turn, took a pinch to the fire. A smaller group walked out into the green meadow, past the deer carcass, and toward the deep green willows alongside Yellow Creek. There they'd plant the two live starts to keep the seeds company and give them encouragement. It's important, the fire maker explained, to have relatives nearby as you take root.

As the seed was tossed, and the plants planted, the ceremony came to an unceremonious close. Beverly Ogle took one of her grandsons by the hand to get him a drink from the soda springs while Lorena Gorbet led the drum circle, all women, in singing: "Walk in beauty, it's all around you."

I've been to protests where shrillness undercut outrage, where decorum undercut meaning. Here casualness underscored something else, something deep and real and unnameable. A little kid pushed a plastic monster truck around the fire as the crowd slowly dispersed. No big pronouncement. No closing procession.

It's not the fact that you protest, I thought, but how.

After the ceremony, cars and trucks bumped slowly up the dusty road toward the campground. One crew lifted the metal fire pit—fire still burning within—with leather gloves into the back of a Dodge Ram. They sat in back to hold it steady. I hopped in a BMW with a couple who owned a vacation cabin nearby. They'd traveled that morning from Chico, some four hours away, to support the Maidu. Beverly had more friends and allies than I had imagined. We passed two small boys hitchhiking along the road—bravely waving their thumbs in the air here where it's safe—and the driver offered them a ride, but they declined. They hopped, instead, in the back of the pickup behind us. Maybe it was someone they knew. Or maybe they just preferred to be truck-bed anonymous, rather than sedan-seat interrogated.

At the reserved campsite, the potluck was taking shape. Wares for sale appeared on blankets: beadwork and T-shirts and photocopied maps of Humbug Valley with its Maidu name: Tasmam Koyom. I went looking for a way to cut a watermelon and met potluckers roasting meat on a rotisserie who were happy to loan a knife and a clean cutting board and talk about the land reclamation. Some had heard I wrote a book about the civil rights movement and expounded on how this story was the same: oppressed people rising up triumphant. One exuberant man, tan and white-bearded, showed me a fir-needle necklace a Maidu friend made him twenty years ago.

He gestured toward the horizon.

"This is huge," he said. "Farrell says this could be Maidu National Park."

The clear-cut was out of sight and apparently out of mind as well. It was as though, once healing acts had been performed, the business of celebrating took over.

Beverly Ogle's youngest son, Ken Holbrook, stood watching his two small kids walk a silver log across the creek, then grinned, set down his keys in the dirt, adjusted his camera strap backwards over his shoulder, and followed them.

Trina Cunningham stood beside me as the three of them balanced.

"Wouldn't it make a great picture to have everyone stand out on the log?" she asked.

"Yeah," I said. "And if you fall in, it's no big deal."

"Right," she said.

I meant the depth—the creek was shallow enough that even a child could stand in the sand and breathe fine—but she meant more.

"We've spent our whole lives in rivers," she said. "We're not afraid."

A white man with a shock of John Kerry hair and a corgi on a leash mingled vigorously. I knew who he was: Edwin Wilson, the lawyer for the tribe in the land negotiations. I loitered, trying to catch his attention, uncertain about his motives. Who was paying him? How committed was he? But before I could catch him, it was time to eat.

The crowd gathered in a large circle while Farrell Cunningham walked along three tables of food and filled a plate with a modest portion from each dish. No one else approached the food. He took his time. Someone said meat was still cooking on a rotisserie, so Farrell stood and waited for it to be done, and everyone waited with him. When at last the meat appeared, he added a piece to his plate, and stood beside the still-burning fire. He thanked everyone for the dishes they brought, gave a blessing, and dumped the entire contents of the plate into the fire as an offering to the spirits of the ancestors who linger in the valley.

People were ready to eat, but Farrell was not finished.

"Since I speak the language, I can give a bit of advice too," he said, half-joking, self-deprecating.

"Don't take too much," he said. "Don't waste food."

After all, these are people's gifts, he said. He goes to too many potlucks where he sees food in the trash. Don't do that, he said. Don't be like that. He tossed in a Maidu phrase with a sly grin, and then translated the meaning: "Don't act like white people."

Everyone laughed.

"Don't take it personally. We're all Maidu here today. But I think you know what I mean."

He gave one last direction before stepping out of the way.

"Elders should eat first," he said. "It's a form of respect. And the young ones, the teenagers here, well, they should find an elder and offer to make a plate."

A small round Maidu boy standing beside me asked shyly if he could make me a plate. I laughed. I was forty-five, not seventy-five, but the boy's gesture was so well-meaning that I felt bad when I turned him down and he slunk away.

I carried my plate, piled high but not too high, and stood beside Farrell Cunningham, standing by himself in the shade of the pines. We ate in comfortable silence. After a while, I asked him how he learned the language.

"At gatherings just like this," he said.

From his aunts, his elders, he said. He preferred their company. He doesn't know why; maybe he was a weird kid, or maybe it was just that they made him laugh. They had a wicked sense of humor, these women, and maybe because of everything they'd been through, boarding school and all the rest, they were irreverent, rebellious, ribald even. He sat with them, always, and they'd speak in Maidu to say rude things and didn't realize that young Farrell could understand.

"I've never met anyone with a sense of humor like that. I can't even describe it."

His face softened as he remembered them. His eyes twinkled under his heavy brow. His voice lost its tinge of sadness.

"This," he said, gesturing around, "is nothing like it was. So polite."

Then as if he regretted having said this, he gestured toward the place where Lorena Gorbet sat selling her beadwork at a card table and Beverly Ogle sat nearby in a lawn chair greeting yet another well-wisher.

"They're charismatic, aren't they?"

"They are," I said.

We ate in silence again.

Two young men approached, exuberantly waving a fork in the air.

"What's the word for this?" one asked.

Farrell gamely played along, told them the word, and that it comes from the verb "to stab."

When they left, he said he's teaching language classes once a month, that he enjoys it and that he visits the elders who remain, some who are housebound, and they talk together in Maidu. He'd finished his food and was growing more talkative.

One of the men returned, excited like a child.

"What's the word for 'welcome'?" he asked.

Farrell thought for a moment. There wasn't one, he said at last. There was a word that meant "go away" but not one for "welcome."

He repeated the word with feeling, a deep bellowing growl. "Go away! Go someplace else!"

You could hear the echo of his aunts' sense of humor, but no malice. He didn't mean I should go away, and he didn't mean the two young men should go away. Not necessarily. He just meant that's how the language works. He laughed soundlessly as he returned to his food.

A young mother nearby shepherded a gang of kids making a pinecone palace, collecting them in one area, placing flowers atop. One little boy preferred to play in an outhouse and she had to keep chasing him. I watched her, and as I did, I saw Edwin Wilson heading across the campground. I followed him to a picnic table near my campsite and realized that he and his family had been the noisy late-night campers. Now they were planning to go fishing in the creek. But when I told him who I was, he sat amiably.

"Do you have time for a story?" he asked.

I did.

"I see it in Michener terms." A long story, he meant. With a wide-angle lens. And an overarching theme. "This was all meant to be," he began.

He told me how grew up in the heart of Maidu country, in Belden Town directly downstream from Humbug Valley—the place where the neon martini glass hovers over the river, the place where Yellow Creek meets the Feather—how he'd grown up with Maidu, he's sure of it, but didn't know them well, didn't realize it, in a way. What he cared about was being outdoors. As a boy he'd follow Yellow Creek upstream, and as a teenager he discovered Humbug Valley, a special place, his very own special place, and as an adult he'd return from his career as a forester and an environmental lawyer in the Bay Area, for solace, for recreation, and still he never knew about the Maidu history until one day when he stumbled upon Beverly Ogle's book in a store in Chester on his way to the campground. When he arrived, he asked a young girl about the book, if she'd ever heard of it, or heard of Ogle.

"Oh, that's my mom," the girl said. "She's right over there."

Since then, Wilson has worked for the Maidu for years pro bono.

"See?" he said. "It was meant to be."

"Do you know why no dam ever went in up here?" he asked.

I'd heard there wasn't enough water, I said. I'd read that. No, he argued, there was plenty of water, there was a plan for where the dam would go, how it would work. There's even a map—Beverly Ogle has it—from 1911 that shows the area, the Maidu sites, the homesteads, topography, and the plans for flooding it all. He knows it's true because when he was a kid hiking up Yellow Creek he'd seen foundations for a railroad line to bring the equipment in. He'd played on them. Why then didn't it happen? He asked me again. He didn't wait for me to reply.

"Because it was meant to be," he said. "Look. You don't have to tell children what's beautiful or what's ugly. You can see the magic, feel it."

He was on a roll. He was passionate. He repeated what I'd heard earlier, how this could be a first, how Farrell Cunningham had spread the word that this could become Maidu National Park. It could set a precedent. I knew plans were afoot elsewhere for national parks to be managed by Indians at least in part. Badlands in South Dakota for one. But those would not be owned by the Indians; they were not so much reclaimed as on loan. It was hard for me to imagine it meant the same thing this did.

"Do you know how the Maidu proved archaeological sites had been damaged by this logging?" Wilson asked.

I did not.

"The 1911 map! The map the power company made when they surveyed for a potential dam. The map Beverly Ogle owns."

He laughed uproariously.

"Even that, even *this*," he said, gesturing toward the logged-over slope, "is meant to be."

Wilson is convinced that PG&E's bad behavior and the resulting bad press will lead to a good outcome. By the end of the year, he said, the tribe will take fee-simple title and reclaim the valley. He is sure of it, but he leans forward to tell me one last thing. He does not believe that the Maidu believe it will happen. Not really, not fully.

I knew what he meant. I could sense this in the Maidu I'd met: hope without hope, faith without faith. Beverly Ogle and Lorena Gorbet and Farrell Cunningham worked tirelessly and with a sense of righteousness, but seemingly without expectation, as though nothing could be counted on, nothing could be assumed, as though anything could change at any time. And of course, it can. As late afternoon sun glinted off the short pole on which an American flag was mounted at the campground entrance, as trucks and vans crept away in a cloud of dust, I wondered if that's exactly what we're missing, me and Edwin Wilson and white people everywhere. I wondered if that earth-solid perspective—baffling, frustrating, and true—is part of what's been gifted to the Maidu.

The day was getting late. I'd already overstayed my camping permit, so I thanked Edwin Wilson and went to take down my tent. A moment later he chased after me. He wanted to say one more thing.

"One more Michener thing. One more big-picture detail. And this is important. Humbug Valley is the last of the great Maidu valleys," he said.

He went on to explain that Big Meadows, Mountain Meadows, Buck Lake, Butte Lake are all drowned while American Valley and Indian Valley have been developed into Quincy and Greenville respectively. Only this one remains unscathed.

"Only Humbug remains," he said.

I thanked him again and walked through the pines to say good-bye to Beverly and a large group of friends and family crowded around a picnic table beside Yellow Creek with dogs by their feet. I'd come as a writer thinking I could help somehow by telling their story, but I was leaving as something else, if not quite a friend, a member of the clan, a humble participant in a story I couldn't yet understand, and maybe never would: a complex web of land and ancestors, Creator and creation, community and responsibility. Fred and Brenda and others rose to offer hugs, to wish me well, and I walked around to Beverly so she wouldn't have to stand. She looked very tired.

"It's been a good day," I said.

"Come back soon," she said.

The logging roads twisted back down to meet asphalt at the junction with US 89, where I turned south, to take a different route, one that led me past the outlet of Lake Almanor, dry in early summer as the reservoir fills with snowmelt. I stopped to take it in: the great exposed slabs of concrete, the sunburned swimmers on the shore, the smell of barbecue, and the great Maidu valley drowned beneath it all. Whatever saved Humbug Valley—the map-corner obscurity, the ancestral spirits, or the charismatic warriors, the tireless reclaimers—I could not be anything but grateful. I rolled the windows down and took the curves slow along the Feather River, with classic rock blaring, barely tolerable, but fitting again, maybe even meant to be: Supertramp's "Take the Long Way Home."

16

No Difference at All

Bishop, California—June 2013

The morning was hot. The temperature was creeping into the mid-nineties before ten. On the outskirts of Bishop, three workers on a small red tractor harvested hay while tank-topped tourists in shiny pickups bought ice at mini-marts on their way to camp and fish, and above it all the mountains hovered, impossibly tall. Mount Whitney, the highest point in the Lower 48, stands at 14,505 feet above sea level southwest of town, and Death Valley, with the lowest point in the Lower 48 at 282 feet below sea level, lies to the southeast. Bishop, the largest town in Inyo County, with a population just under 4,000 and elevation just over 4,000 feet, splits the difference with desert temps and mountain views and on Main Street a dozen cheap chain motels.

My destination, three blocks off the main drag, turned out to be more office complex than strip mall, two stories in paint-faded blue. The parking lot was full of cars. One glass door had the Timbisha Shoshone name stenciled on it with an elaborate logo. Even when I set aside two full days, dressed in an ironed shirt, and packed my digital recorder, I had not expected this.

The night before, I'd returned from Humbug Valley to my friends' house and regaled the family with stories of the healing ceremony and the potluck and the kid who'd wanted to fix me an elder plate. I couldn't contain my excitement. Then I told them about my plan to head to Bishop, how different it would be to meet George Gholson, the Timbisha tribal council chairman, how I worried that he would be a genuine bad guy, a crook, a pawn of casino developers. I even wondered if he'd be dangerous.

My friend wanted to see a picture, so together we googled Gholson and stumbled upon a video of a council meeting, the first image of the man I'd seen. Several Timbisha I'd spoken with in Furnace Creek had described him to me as "white" or "almost white" and suggested that he was up to no good—shutting down offices in Death Valley, prioritizing a casino over other needs, rigging enrollment to assure his own election—so I'd expected a slick operator, someone in a suit with a faux Rolex or maybe gold chains. Instead, Gholson looked like any rural politician, a regular guy behind a folding table at a meeting: heavyset and unsmiling in a polo shirt and slacks. He also looked distinctly Native. But regular guy or not, he was not easy to chase down.

In the morning I called to leave a message, to tell him again that I planned to be in Bishop that day. A woman picked up.

"Who's calling?" she asked.

I said my full name.

"With?"

I said that I was a writer and I'd been trying to reach Mr. Gholson for months.

"Oh, okay," she said and put me through to voice mail.

So I got in the car and drove four hours south.

Google Earth showed one address for the Bishop, California, tribal offices to be a suburban rambler. Maybe it was a front, I thought. Maybe there was no tribal office at all. Another address showed a strip mall in which the individual businesses were too blurry to distinguish. I did not want to risk showing up at someone's home, so I tried the strip mall first.

Now I sat sweltering in the rental car and watched as a large Native woman, perhaps the woman on the phone, walked out of the office. No use waiting. I grabbed my bag and hurried in. A blast of air-conditioning greeted me in the foyer, and a loud door-triggered bell announced my arrival. The place seemed officious enough. A large empty front desk held racks of business cards for all council members and forms for housing assistance and a sign-in sheet on a clipboard. The sheet was nearly full. I signed in. I called out tentatively, received no answer, and followed a narrow hallway past windowless offices until I found one occupied. A polite older gentlemen told me Mr. Gholson was busy and ushered me quickly back out to the foyer, where a new receptionist, a young white woman, took me back through the morning interrogation.

"Can I help you?"

"Can I speak with Mr. Gholson?"

"Who is asking?"

"Ana Maria Spagna."

"From?"

"Washington State."

My reply was part coy, part exasperation, but she accepted it and hit an intercom.

Then he appeared, walking very slowly. He wore a Bluetooth earpiece and held a smartphone and did not make eye contact. I introduced myself.

"I've been trying to contact you to talk about the Homeland Act for several months."

I reached out my hand, but he ignored it.

"Maybe once or twice," he said.

"I wonder if there's time for us to talk today or tomorrow."

He scrolled through his phone with his thumb.

"Three thirty this afternoon."

He did not look up.

"Great," I said. "I'll see you then."

He paused.

"No. It better be tomorrow," he said.

He began to speak softly to the receptionist in phrases heavy on acronyms that I could not discern. I reached in front of him, between them, to take one of his business cards, flipped it over and held a pen ready.

"What time tomorrow?"

"Ten."

I wrote that down and waited for him to reciprocate. I showed him the sign-in sheet with the spelling of my name, but he wrote nothing down. I opened the door to a shock of heat like a sock in the chest and pulled away to while away the afternoon, camp near town for the night, and await the morning meeting. I did not for a second believe he'd show up.

The Homeland Act was thirteen years old. The victory had been won, but all those laudatory articles in scholarly journals and books on Indian law and national park history seemed as removed from here as the stark landscape of Furnace Creek. Every reclamation has its aftermath. On NPR on the drive down I'd listened to a story from the Elwha, where nearly 200,000 salmon and steelhead, set to be released in the river after the dam removals, had been accidentally killed off when a pump failed. Lawsuits were pending. The Timbisha had their share of lawsuits, too. Thirteen years' worth. At least seven bank accounts had been opened then subsequently frozen due to the rift between the Bishop faction and the Death Valley faction. Exasperated federal officials sounded condescending in their decisions. The latest, a rejection of a federal court appeal, summarized the situation: "The Kennedy faction is unhappy with how the election was run, who voted, and who won, but ours is not the forum for that debate. . . . It is bedrock principle that every tribe is capable of managing its own affairs and governing itself." Maybe the tribe had not shown itself capable, not yet, but some of what I'd seen in the strip mall office had seemed hopeful: the assistance forms, the full sign-in sheet, the sheer number of offices and employees. Someone was apparently doing all right.

The next morning George Gholson stood in the same spot by the front reception desk where I'd seen him last, leaning on his forearms, staring at his phone. He did not look up.

"You're five minutes early," he said.

"Yes," I said.

He left the room.

The receptionist, the third I'd seen in two days, brought me an ice-cold plastic bottle of Dasani water, and I asked her about the logo on the door.

"Do you know anything about it?"

It looked like a snake with a basket, but it couldn't be a snake, according to what Pauline Esteves had told me. She claimed the Timbisha historically didn't even say the word "rattlesnake." The receptionist thought it must be some plant, dried and wrapped perhaps, like a sage smudge or a wreath. The problem was they only had half the logo since they did not have permission to use the rest of it.

"Due to the infighting," she said.

The fact that she acknowledged the rift so matter-of-factly came as a relief. Beside the desk, a large glass case showcased Timbisha-Shoshone T-shirts and baseball caps with the half-logo, and a collection of fine small baskets labeled "Panamint-Shoshone." The receptionist explained they'd been made by George Gholson's relatives, and this led to her own heritage, Mexican American, and how she'd learned to make tamales from her grandmother. I was getting ready to ask about this discrepancy in the tribal name, Panamint versus Timbisha, when, at ten o'clock sharp, George Gholson appeared again.

He walked me to a large conference room equipped with microphone hookups and a large flat-screen monitor. He pulled up a chair kitty-corner from me, opened his own sweaty bottle of Dasani, and made eye contact for the first time, his eyes dark brown, his lips full, his teeth a little crooked. He kept the Bluetooth in his ear.

"Do you mind if I record?" I asked.

"Not at all," he said.

I launched into my spiel about reclamation and how the Homeland Act was such a victory. "At least that's how it seems from the outside," I said.

I caught the edge of his rueful smile.

"I'm wondering, from the inside, what has changed as a result?"

He did not miss a beat.

"You know what has changed? Nothing."

He had rehearsed this line and expected some shock. I showed none. I felt none. "We still have substandard housing, substandard roads, no economic development."

He'd repeat this phrase—"economic development"—a dozen times over the course of our one-hour conversation.

"Why?"

The reacquired lands are too isolated to develop. Only Furnace Creek would be good for anything, due to the tourists, and even when you think you own it, guess what? You don't. You want to make any changes, you gotta jump through all the environmental hoops, you gotta ask permission from the BIA, from the EPA, from the Park Service. That's what happened to him, to them, he said, when they tried to replace a few power poles in Indian Village.

"But you got them?"

"We eventuuuuuuuaaallly got them," he said. His enunciation leaned Comedy Central: incredulous, slightly mocking, slightly Hispanic. Not far from the way Pauline Esteves sounded when she'd say "ridiculous."

"What about the people who worked so hard to pass the Homeland Act? What were they looking for? Did they get it?"

"See, that's where I'm confused. I don't know what they were looking for. I don't think they were thinking of the future, or if they had a vision for the future."

I knew they had a vision, one that was land-based, steeped in culture and tradition. I tried to steer the conversation toward common ground. What about a hotel in Furnace Creek? A modest eco-tourism sort of place?

That'd be great, he said with a shrug, but it was not realistic.

"Native Americans are not entrepreneurs. They're not capitalists. But the younger generations are starting to learn."

He clearly considered himself in the latter group though his black buzz cut was flecked with gray.

"I myself wasn't raised on a reservation. I was raised in Grants, New Mexico. Uranium capital of the world. My dad was a chemist and he worked in the industry for thirty-five years or something, so we didn't grow up anywhere near reservation life. My mom did not want us to be Indians."

This, I thought, might explain why other Timbisha dismissed Gholson as "white"—not skin color but attitude. Still, considering the living conditions on most reservations, you could see why a mother would make such a choice.

"So I'm not in touch with that, which I think gives me a unique perspective as chairman as to what the tribe needs to do in today's environment."

"And you face resistance?"

"Oh, huuuuuuge resistance. There's a big fear of change, like we're going to take something away. I don't know what the reasoning is. Everyone's afraid of change until it's done. Then it's like: We should've done this years ago. See, there's a portion of the tribe that's out in the world. They have houses and they have their kids and grandkids. Those folks understand economic development. Then you have the people who have never experienced that."

"Do you think they don't want to?"

"I think it's like if you never had electricity, you wouldn't miss it. They've never had the jobs, the cars, the house, the ability to manage their finances, so it's just something they're not going to miss."

I asked about his mother's people. "Is that where your Timbisha blood comes from?"

"Yeah. Panamint Shoshone. The word 'Timbisha' didn't show up until the recognition, but all the documentation I've seen is Panamint Shoshone."

I remembered the film in Furnace Creek, how Barbara Durham described how the word Timbisha referred to the red stone in Death Valley.

"Are your mother's people from Death Valley?" I asked.

"No, they were down south of Lone Pine, mostly in the coastal mountain range which is now China Lake Naval Weapons Station," he said.

He repeated the familiar refrain that the tribe had always moved seasonally—winter in the desert, summer in the mountains—and he added another dimension. They had to move, he said, because the history of Indians in California is so particularly dreadful. His mother had told him stories she heard from her mother.

"If you left one place, and didn't take your kids with you, when you came back you found them in pieces in the trees."

Pauline Esteves's house was burned down in the 1960s because she left in summer. Not as dramatic as kids in pieces in trees, but there was truth to what he said, I knew. Migration wasn't just dictated by weather.

"In today's society, we cannot imagine that ever happening. You think about these European countries that have mass graves and atrocities that have happened fairly recently, then you look at America and it's just so far out there. You take your average American and they're gonna be like: Noooo way. Didn't happen. Even myself, even though my family is part of it, I can't believe it."

"Do you think it's because of that history that some of the elders are so concerned about change?"

"Yeah, they call it historical trauma. But I myself I don't feel the historical trauma."

I sat scribbling in a notebook—to look busy, to give him time to elaborate—and thinking: Maybe that's part of what I'd been missing about reclaimers. If you don't feel the trauma, you don't feel the connection. For some people, loss creates a need for reclamation, grief leads to action.

"What about the old ways?" I asked. "What about the harvesting rights outlined in the Homeland Act?"

He waved his hand before his face, like batting a swarm of gnats.

"Culture is always evolving. It has to. What was considered 'culture' before was just a way of life. It's how you survived. And culture today is going to be different."

"What about the grinding of mesquite or the pine nut collecting?"

"Those were like going to Albertson's today. You did that to live."

Nowadays, he said, Indians have opportunities to move away from all that, to improve themselves. They can attend Bishop Community College, for example, and the Owens Valley Career Development Center will pay for everything. Books, tuition, everything. He said he's doing it himself, getting a degree in human services.

"If that wasn't on the reservation there'd be a line around the building. There's nobody there. Now I've had student loans, and I've lived in the dorms and ate nothing and had to work, and I know what you go through with that. My wife and I were married with two kids, and I was going to school, and she was going to school, and it's no picnic. But to be able to come to a place like this and get a two-year degree . . ." He shook his head. "Even when there are jobs for the taking, like these in the office, there aren't qualified tribal members to fill them," he said. "Sometimes no Indians at all."

He paused, slouched back in his chair, and sipped his water. I thought about Barbara Durham. She'd been to college, two colleges in fact, but she came home to Death Valley to negotiate for the Homeland Act, to fight for it. She was certainly qualified for a job. She'd even had a job, as tribal historic preservation officer, until it was yanked from her. I wondered how things were for her now; I made a mental note to ask George Gholson about that. But not yet.

"See what I'm saying?" he said. "No difference at all."

He joked that China Lake, the naval weapons facility, is, in many ways, his homeland.

"Things there are protected, too . . . and bombed," he said.

Gholson had a keen sense of irony; he was smart and likable, and he was gaining steam as we talked. My head was beginning to swirl. Was he such a bad guy after all?

"What about the casino? Are there still plans in the works?"

"Yeah, we're still trying to work on something. That's one of our primary goals. But it's tough, it's tough. The Indian gaming has come to the forefront, so people are watching us more."

"Is most of the resistance to gaming from outside the tribe or within the tribe?"

"Oh, outside. And sometimes from other tribes."

"Because it's competition?"

"Yeah. Which from an economic standpoint makes sense."

"What do you think the probability is that it will happen?"

"I think it's a long shot. It comes down to the Golden Rule: The people with the gold make the rules."

I laughed. I could imagine some Timbisha members saying precisely this about him. Still I wanted to be clear about what he was saying.

"So if the tribe had taken all the energy they put into passing the Homeland Act and put it into gaming to start with, would you be better off?"

"To a degree, but I think the tribe was not mature or prepared."

"What do you mean?"

"If you take the U.S. government as a model and look at the Revolutionary War and the laws and the formation of the government, and how long it took. Well, the Timbisha are just now developing a constitution."

"You're a young nation," I said.

"Yes, exactly. So I think when it came to the casino we were mostly ignorant and susceptible to manipulation."

"Do you think that happened?"

"Yes, definitely. You take a group of people who don't have money and throw money at them, they aren't going to know what to do with it. And that's exactly what happened. And that's when the fighting started, and it's been a decade, and we're just getting over it. We still have a lot of fence-mending to do."

"What about Barbara Durham?" I asked at last. "Is she working for the tribe these days?"

"Yes," he said. "The offices in Death Valley are open." He did not elaborate.

I gazed at the large flat-screen TV that dominated the conference room where we sat and wondered how it might be used. For tribal members Skyping in to council meetings? That did not seem in keeping with the picture of a poor uneducated people in the desert. But, of course, they don't all live in the desert. Gholson boasted that tribal members live "from coast to coast, border to border," with one in living in Japan, one in South America. Less than 5 percent of the tribe lives in Death Valley. He argued for inclusiveness, for modernity, for economic development. I sat listening, feeling lulled into the reasonableness of his arguments, until suddenly from nowhere, mid-conversation, I felt a shiver.

His arguments seemed dangerously close to ones that have wreaked havoc for three hundred years. From broken treaties in the early 1800s to allotment in the 1880s to termination in the 1950s, damaging policy has so often stemmed from this basic premise: Get with the program. I'd recently watched a Fox News special that claimed Indians were the most subsidized group in America. The program featured footage of reservation squalor, stray dogs and barefoot children, drunken toothless men, as if to say: This is what happens when the government gives everything to you. But that is not true. It's what happens when the government has taken everything from you, when you survive genocide, and are trying to figure out how to live now.

I asked how his day looked, and he said busy. Every day is busy.

Before I left I asked what he'd done before becoming council chair.

"What didn't I do?"

He was a radio man in the navy, stationed in England at a base run by the Royal Air Force. He'd worked as a mechanic and a truck driver and an accountant. Now, in addition to his position as tribal chairperson, he owned an audiovisual equipment and setup company and did karaoke.

"Karaoke? You set it up?"

"Yeah, and sing."

On my way out I stopped again to admire the Panamint baskets, and he stopped beside me to explain that these treasures had been discovered by accident by a tribal member at an auction in Reno, and the basket makers were indeed his relatives. May Davis was Gholson's grandmother, and Mary Gregory his great-aunt. He was pleased by them, excited even, but he said when his great-grandmother tried to teach him as a kid he "wasn't smart enough" to want to learn.

I turned toward the door.

"Oh, one more thing. What's that on the logo? Is that some kind of sage?"

"No," he said, "It's a digging stick."

"Right. It looks like a snake, but I knew it couldn't be a snake."

"Oh, it could. Some people say Shoshone means snake."

Later I'd learn that Lewis and Clark had in fact called the Shoshone people—the people from whom they recruited Sacajawea—the "Snake People," but the Indians themselves translated the word to mean "the Valley People" or "the Inland People." The fact that Gholson accepted the Lewis and Clark definition seemed right; in a way he accepted the Fox News party line, too. He'd sided with the victors. And it was hard to fault him. You need only to look at the fate of Lewis and Clark's cultural descendants versus those of Sacajawea to see that Gholson is a realist.

I left the air-conditioned office and raced to the air-conditioned car and headed to a coffee shop to call Barbara Durham. I could not wait to double-check Gholson's story.

I told her he'd told me she had her job back and that everything was "more or less hunky-dory."

She laughed. "Good things have happened," she said. Jobs had opened down there, and local people were filling them. They were getting along with the Park Service, and a Death Valley conservation group had offered to buy two museum-quality display cases to use for the baskets.

"I saw them," I said. "They're beautiful."

She explained excitedly that she found the baskets in Reno while attending a conference, that she's the one who called George Gholson and got him to hightail it up there to make a bid.

They were working together as best they could, mending fences.

I wished her a good weekend. She said she heard it was going to get hot, real hot. The forecast was for highs of 123 degrees Fahrenheit. What would she do then?

"I'll just sit in the dark by the swamp cooler," she said.

I imagined Barbara Durham sitting in Furnace Creek, holding her ground in the homeland, siding with patience, while George Gholson headed to a cool dark bar to sing someone else's song.

Coda

The High Ground

Winter solstice nears. Along the lake this morning I counted nine trumpeter swans among the buffleheads and coots. At home, my footprints have melted to dirt in two inches of crusty snow. If I look out the window, I can watch different-colored flagging flutter on trees: three possible routes for the new road, one very close, one medium, and one farther back. The flagging has hung for a long time now, long enough for the colors to fade, but work has yet to begin. There's a squeeze on government spending, temporary or long-term no one knows, then there's compliance to be completed, the labyrinth of regulations and safeguards that must be navigated before any public project that can conceivably impact the environment can go forward. There's even a rumor, yet to be substantiated, that the Yakama Nation is involved now, exerting its power to assure the proper archaeological studies have been completed. Whether the road will ever be constructed on the high ground seems up in the air. Whether another flood will tear through the low ground first, we can't say. We planted dogwoods and cedars, hoping the roots will take hold before the river tugs at them. Someday soon we plan to tether a half-dozen root balls—excavated stumps with roots attached—against the bank to protect it and to double later as fish habitat. Or maybe, as friends half-jokingly suggest, we'll line the bank with rusted hulls of abandoned cars, never a shortage in a place like this, to do the same thing. The lessons of my journey are sinking in. Do what you can. Hope without hope. Expect the unexpected.

One night in August an email arrived from Beverly Ogle's son Fred Mankins. He'd been writing regularly; he was working with PG&E to use the principles of TEK in Humbug Valley, and he was excited to keep me up-to-date on the projects. But this email was different. The subject line read "A Tribe of Broken Hearts." This did not seem like Fred, or really, like any of the Maidu. I'd corresponded a couple days earlier with the lawyer, Edwin Wilson, who assured me that progress with PG&E was steady, that the land reclamation would happen by September. I opened the email.

Farrell Cunningham was dead. He'd been found alone in his house, a death from natural causes, though it's hard to accept a thirty-seven-year-old man's death as natural, especially this man's. The obituaries trickled in slowly over the next few weeks, filled with surprising details. Farrell spoke seven languages. He wrote and painted and taught and gardened and sometimes raged. I'd met the man once and I knew this much: he felt the loss of his ancestors and their language personally, and he tried to keep it alive, and he felt the burden that came with it, too. The loss would be devastating. There'd be no way to overstate it. None of the condolences I tried to offer made a whit of difference. On the phone, Beverly Ogle sounded resigned. This is what you must anticipate: what you never dare anticipate.

On the Columbia River a crack appeared in Wanapum Dam, two dams downstream from Rocky Reach. The crack in a spillway pillar was found to be the result of a design error fifty years ago when the dam went in, and repair estimates were placed at $69 million. To alleviate pressure on the underwater crack, the river behind the dam was drawn down twenty-six feet, leaving orchardists in a panic. While they could extend their irrigation pipes to reach the lowered water level easily enough, there wasn't enough time to refit those pipes with the required and expensive fish screening before the dry season. Meanwhile, the drawdown exposed miles of new beaches and banks, coated in dry cracking mud, and dozens of Indian gravesites and potentially thousands of artifacts. People flocked to see what they could see, what'd been lost, what'd been under the surface, and police tried to turn them away without much luck. Three people got stuck in the mud and had to be rescued.

Just up the road in Quincy, Washington, where crop names line the fences along the highway into town—corn, potatoes, alfalfa, apples, wheat—and a Mexican grocery dominates the main intersection, a whole slew of oversized data centers that look a lot like trucking warehouses have sprouted up. Sabey, Yahoo, Microsoft, and Intuit all chose the place because the power source is reliable—there are hardly ever outages this close to the source—and because they can buy electricity at less than half the cost of the national average and use it to maintain climate-controlled storage for our cute kitten photos and on-demand music collections. The definition of useful stretches and morphs and sometimes disappoints. But I have a friend as skilled in the woods as anyone you'll meet, a guy who can jerry-rig a wall tent with saplings and a tarp or guide a raft or fight fire or pull enough fish from a creek to feed a small campfire crowd. After years as a seasonal Forest Service employee, he went back to school to train in heating and air conditioning maintenance and got a job at a data center that's a thousand times better than any he had before. Good pay, benefits, and plenty of time off. Is the data center useful to him? It is.

On the White Salmon River, rafters and kayakers head down the newly opened section of whitewater. On YouTube, you can watch the colorful boats with helmeted passengers bob and spin and plummet. The gorge, a collapsed lava tube, is so narrow in places the boats must take turns single file, and there's still hardly enough room. When at last they pass the dam site, there's nothing, nothing at all, to suggest the mammoth structure was ever there. The narrators express awe at how fast nature has recovered. The revegetation is growing, the sediment is being scoured away, and salmon are returning to the river and side channels, preparing redds, laying eggs, even as scientists measure the extent of mortality of other species, the ones that aren't anadromous like salmon, the ones that live in the river all the time, or used to.

Reclaimers

At some point the question of scale arises. Aren't the benefits and consequences of building or removing or raising a dam more dramatic, and therefore more critical, than how, when, or where to harvest bear grass? The stakes are higher, people argue, hands wringing, all out of proportion to what we humans have dealt with before. But there's the scale of time to consider, too. When I finally spoke with Kat Anderson about her book *Tending the Wild*, I asked her how long the concept of traditional ecological knowledge has been around. She misunderstood my question, or more precisely, she answered a more cogent one. Basketry has been around for 45,000 years, she said. It's fair to assume humans have known how to tend plants for that purpose for at least that long, a practice—call it an art or a science or, perhaps most appropriately, a relationship—that's been honed through trial and error for millennia. We can't claim reclaiming is a new and daunting task.

The question applies to thinking, too. Reclamation requires thinking big: Charles Wilkinson asking the Timbisha negotiators and the Park Service officials about their dreams, Edwin Wilson describing the Maidu saga in Michener terms. But it also requires thinking small, one place at a time, one relationship at a time, one plant at a time.

The pervasive belief that we can't think both ways at once—it's big or small, black or white, yin or yang, male or female, inside or outside—is, of course, nonsense, what Pauline Esteves might call ridiculous. We do it all the time, or the best of us do. Charles Wilkinson urged people to talk about their dreams, then facilitated painstaking negotiations. J. D. Ross championed public power, then designed valves to prevent excessive siltation. Jeff Osborn defended endangered species policy, then took people outside to see real live chinook salmon writhing in the shallows. And while we hear plenty of business-speak along these lines—the need to apply large concepts on the small scale—what's impressive is how often the reverse occurs. Thinking small, acting big. Phyllis Clausen was thinking only of the bucolic river flowing past her weekend home when she called up American Rivers with a radical proposal. Beverly Ogle was putting out rogue campfires as a campground host in Humbug Valley when she crashed in on PG&E's meeting. Pauline Esteves was simply holding on to her home with no running water or electricity, a home that had once been burned right out from under her, when she led her tribe to take land back from the United States of America.

But even that's not the whole of it. There's something deeper. Say Danny Manning's crew starts a fire with matches and pine boughs instead of a drip torch; it's still the same fire, but the attitude is entirely different. They're acknowledging those who came before, acknowledging they're not the first to start such a fire, maybe even accepting responsibility, through intimacy, for whatever the fire may do, good and bad. It's not impossible to imagine we can apply the same reverence to decisions about dams or, say, pipelines.

At the end of *Tending the Wild*, Kat Anderson argues that long-term sustainability will require cultural changes including establishing mores about using too much, reinforcing them with social and spiritual practices—prayer, song, dances, offerings, and taboos—and nurturing a "kincentric" relationship with nature, where plants and animals are seen as brothers and sisters. (Wallace Stegner said essentially the same thing fifty years ago when he argued for the need to preserve wild places so humans remember that we are "brother to the animals, part of the natural world and competent to belong to it.") When I talked with Kat Anderson, she reminded me repeatedly, insistently, that the ideas were never hers. The cumulative wisdom belongs to generations of Native people gathering on the land in a twofold sense: gathering together, hanging out, and gathering what they need. If it seems a modest vision, it's one with staying power, and when it materializes, even today, it feels huge.

When the news arrived, I hopped in the car and drove eight hundred miles south along the east side of the Cascades through thin cold November air tinged with sage and juniper, past cars with missing headlights and smokers in hoodies huddled outside mini-marts and the still-snowy volcanoes—Adams, Hood, Jefferson, Sisters, Shasta—floating over it all. I drove through Lassen Volcanic Park, a high alpine detour, and stopped in a turnout to sit on a slab of granite and gaze down at the wide swath of former Maidu lands. We live in an urban age, or a virtual age, an age when many people want to believe all undeveloped land is either caged up or doomed, but the view from here belied that belief. A soft expanse of forest rolled over ridges, obscuring highways and reservoirs and dwarfing human influence. Maybe it's easier to believe it's all doomed on the grand scale—land, water, flora, fauna—because then we don't have to worry about how to care for it on the small scale. I tried to pick out Humbug Valley, somewhere just west of Lake Almanor, but I could not. From that distance, the sacred valley looked too much like everyplace else.

I landed in Red Bluff at nightfall and set up camp by the Sacramento River with two sleeping bags, a wool cap, and mittens for reading by headlamp, but I couldn't sleep. I got up and walked in the light of the gibbous moon among live oaks, thinking this might be it, the last trip, the end of my journey. The next morning I visited Beverly Ogle at home, brought her a bag of apples I'd picked with my mother in late fall in Stehekin. She sat beside her woodstove surrounded by her unfinished manuscripts, with her children and grandchildren coming and going, and she beamed. Like Martin Luther King Jr., she said, she had a dream.

"Only difference is, I lived to see it come true," she said.

When it was time for the celebration, I drove frantic circles through Chester. I'd failed to write down directions, thinking surely this would be the biggest event in town. I'd just look for the building with all the cars parked out front. But it was Sunday morning, and there were more churches in town than you'd guess, and each church in town had a full parking lot. I stopped at the bookstore to ask directions, figuring bookish locals would be excited about this, but the clerk knew nothing. At last I trailed an old Ford truck down a side street to a newish building beside a park where a group of small kids clambered on rocks under tall pines. A dog I recognized lay unleashed in the sun. This was the right place.

Inside, a crowd mingled. Not as large a crowd as I'd hoped for or expected, but a happy crowd nonetheless, imbued with the same easy camaraderie as the Humbug Valley gathering in summer. Several young men, heavyset with braids and baseball caps and baggy jeans, held squirming kids in their arms. A group of women set their drums in a circle. Potluck dishes accumulated on folding tables, including venison stew and small Dixie cups of acorn paste, a traditional Maidu staple that tastes exactly as you'd imagine: thick, earthy, nutty, slightly bland. I added my own small salad—cherry tomatoes and cukes I'd chopped at a roadside pullout in the sun since it was too cold at my campsite by the river—and went to talk to Beverly's son Ken Holbrook.

In Farrell Cunningham's absence, Ken had been named executive director of the Maidu Summit Consortium, the first ever. He wore a crisp white shirt, gray jeans, and a red tie, the only tie in the room, and he leaned in to tell me a story. He'd recently traveled to a conference in Salamanca, Spain, to present their efforts to reclaim Humbug Valley and their goal of using TEK to manage the land as an example not only for other indigenous people but for land managers everywhere. He also championed the idea of partnerships. When the deal was finalized, the Maidu Summit Consortium would hold fee title to Humbug Valley, but two partners—Feather River Land Trust and the California Department of Fish and Wildlife—would jointly hold a conservation easement. The Land Trust would help determine how much development might be appropriate—improvements in the campground, for instance—then monitor that development. The California Department of Fish and Wildlife would manage the fishery, the pesky non-native brown trout, and the wildlife, including endangered and potentially endangered species like the willow flycatcher and the Sierra red fox. Even PG&E would remain a partner, in a way, a huge one if you consider the financial side of things. The utility company agreed to provide funding for long-term planning and two full-time staff positions, including Ken Holbrook's.

When he spoke about Humbug Valley in Salamanca, Ken said, he stood in the exact same place where Queen Isabella commissioned Christopher Columbus to come to the New World.

"The exact same place," he said.

He told me this story, told anyone who would listen, as though things had come full circle. The symbolism was impossibly seductive, the hopefulness contagious.

When at last formalities began, the first to speak were members of the Maidu Summit Consortium, people who endured years of negotiations, interminable meetings, to get to this point. Their eyes sparkled as they described Humbug Valley and how this moment was meant to be and their hopes for the future.

"This is exactly what I dreamed as a child," Ken Holbrook said.

"I never thought I'd see this day," Lorena Gorbet said.

One woman, impeccably dressed, with the poise of a no-nonsense substitute teacher or perhaps a U.S. senator, was the only speaker to show any hint of anger. She stood, trembling, and approached the microphone.

"I never thought I'd live to see Indians given *anything* by the dominant culture," she said.

The applause was long.

At the end of the speeches, Beverly Ogle's daughter Brenda stood to make a surprise announcement. Well, it was a surprise to Beverly, at least. Her kids had told me about it in her driveway the day before. Beverly was to be awarded a special lifetime achievement award by the Indigenous Communities of Northern California. With it she'd receive a hand-crafted bow. At the celebration, Brenda presented the bow and announced with pride that Beverly Ogle was the first woman ever to receive this award. But, Brenda explained, there were no arrows to go with it. The arrows will come later, next spring, when the Maidu return to Humbug Valley.

As tables were cleared and folding chairs clattered, I moved around the room saying good-bye and stopped to see Beverly last.

"Now the real work begins," she said. "And you'll be back," she added.

I stepped out into fading winter sun with my notes and an empty Tupperware container and drove until dark, from fire-scarred forest to wide dry basin, past small lakes—natural or dammed, it was impossible to tell—and small towns with boarded storefronts and tidy clapboard houses with porch lights on. I thought about home and our uncertain high ground, and I thought about next spring. I'd thought this trip would be the end of it, but I knew the truth: the stories never end.

This much I know: change will come hard and fast—natural disasters and government decisions, dams and oil wells, then smallpox or cancer or a left turn in traffic—and someone somewhere will arrive to reclaim it all, to fill in the gaps. Strangers from over the hills or across the sea or, hell, a faraway galaxy. For now, we are the strangers. And while we're here, we hang on to the remnants, protect the glassy stone chips just under the surface, shovel out the mud, and replant and rebuild the best way we know how.

We're reclaimers by nature.

Acknowledgments

I owe deep gratitude, first, to the many reclaimers who shared with me their stories: their dreams, their ideas, their frustrations, their knowledge, their family histories, and their deep love for the places where they live and work. Some of what they shared appears in these pages, much does not. Every word of it informed my understanding, tweaked it in some way, and changed the way I see the world for the better. For your time, patience, honesty, and inspiration, thank you, Pauline Esteves, Barbara Durham, Grace Goad, Joe Kennedy, Erick Mason, George Gholson, John Reynolds, Dick Martin, Charles Wilkinson, Darrel Jury, Farrell Cunningham, Trina Cunningham, Beverly Ogle, Lorena Gorbet, Edwin Wilson, Fred Mankins, Brenda Heard-Duncan, Ken Holbrook, Danny Manning, Paul Hardy, Kate Bagby, Wade McMaster, Mike Barnhart, Jeff Osborn, Cindy Raekes, Pat Arnold, Phyllis Clausen, and Steve Stampfli.

I'm also indebted to those who helped me get those stories down on the page, to bring them to life, and to make of them some semblance of sense. Thanks to those who read entire drafts, sometimes multiple times, and offered smart and soulful suggestions for improvement: Amanda Skelton, Janet Buttenwieser, Dan Lehman, Jo Scott Coe, Robin Hemley, and Robin Wall Kimmerer. Thanks, too, to the editors who published excerpts with generosity and enthusiasm: Brian Doyle at *Portland*, Michelle Nijhuis at *High Country News*, Hattie Fletcher at *Creative Nonfiction*, Anna Lena Phillips at *Ecotone*, and the editors at *Cutbank*. Thanks to Mesa Refuge in Point Reyes Station, California, for the gifts of time, space, nourishing food, and the acquaintance of one magic red fox. Thanks to all my writer friends—my fabulous colleagues and students at Whidbey Writers Workshop, especially Lisa Tobe, who helped me make crucial connections, my dear loyal Flick Creek friends, the good folks at the River Teeth and Chesapeake conferences, and many others—for camaraderie, commiseration, and the endless inspiration of their own work. Thanks, most especially, to Regan Huff at University of Washington Press for her energetic faith in the book and her care in shepherding it to publication, from a coffee shop in the U District through apple harvest in Stehekin and beyond.

For background material, context, and general elucidation, I turned to many sources, but returned most often to Charles Wilkinson, Jesse Kennedy, Theodore Catton, Jane Braxton-Little, M. Kat Anderson, Beth Rose Middleton, Vine Deloria Jr., and Kathie Durbin.

I owe thanks to Teresa Kulik, Claudia Bertolone Smith, and Sue Spagna for traveling companionship and hospitality, and to my friends and neighbors in Stehekin for keeping me connected to home and connected to my own real non-writer self, and finally, to Laurie, for everything, always.